THE OXFORD OF
INSPECTOR MORSE
══◄═══AND LEWIS══►══

BILL LEONARD

The
History
Press

Colin Dexter with
the sisters of Kenny
McBain who was the
inspiration for the
series.

First published in 2008

The History Press
The Mill, Brimscombe Port,
Stroud, Gloucestershire, GL5 2QG
www.thehistorypress.co.uk

Reprinted 2009 (twice), 2010, 2011, 2012, 2015

British Library Cataloguing in Publication Data.
A catalogue record for this book is available from the British Library.

ISBN 978 0 7524 4621 9

Typesetting and origination by
The History Press Ltd.
Printed in Turkey by Imak.

CONTENTS

FOREWORD

How curiously pleasurable it is to encounter a particular city, a street, a building or whatever, in real life – and later to read about those identical scenes and places in a work of fiction. The converse is also true, since it is equally pleasurable to read about hitherto unknown sights and sites, and only thereafter personally to visit the scenes that have been thus described.

There are those of us who know the beautiful city of Oxford fairly intimately and who thoroughly relish the description of well-remembered streets, etc. There are many others, knowing little or nothing of Oxford, who were first captivated by the depiction of it either in books or on TV. And without doubt the filming of the *Inspector Morse* series has brought countless visitors and tourists to see for themselves what the city has to offer. Indeed a good many viewers have expressed to me their disappointment that a few of the *Morse* episodes were not filmed in Oxford. It is as if the physical presence of the city itself had assumed a major role in the whole proceedings, contributing hugely to viewers' enjoyment.

In *The Oxford of Inspector Morse*, Bill Leonard presents us with a splendidly researched and illustrated review of all the places connected with the Morse books and TV programmes. It is a delightful and fascinating guide, and one which will become a 'must' for those wishing to trace the steps of the enigmatic chief inspector.

I have always admitted that my knowledge of police investigation is virtually nil, with any rare bits of official procedure gleaned almost invariably from the novels of my fellow crime-writers. In compensation for this, I have claimed that my topographical knowledge of Oxford is usually fairly good, and I believe that readers of my books could very easily follow the directions and routes as indicated in the text without being led up too many blind alleys. Bill Leonard has beaten me on all counts.

The only thing that is not answered here is the sort of question put to me more frequently than any other: why, say, when Morse leaves the Radcliffe Infirmary and turns left into Woodstock Road does he immediately find himself in the middle of the High Street? The answer is surprisingly simple. Parking! The difficulty (impossibility) of parking half a dozen TV vans outside a preferred location led to all sorts of problems for us – including, for example, shooting a scene inside one college quad, and shooting the exit of that scene from the porters' lodge of a different college. But I mustn't give too many secrets away.

I shall treasure this guide, and I hope that many others will do the same.

Colin Dexter

INTRODUCTION

A frequent question put to an Oxford guide in one of the college quadrangles, is whether the race in *The Chariots of Fire* was filmed here (the answer is no, the actual race was at Trinity College, Cambridge, and the film was made at Eton College). This obscure event has stirred the imagination of millions of viewers, and the skill of the filmmakers has enhanced interest in both these places. People like to see sites that have inspired creative artists.

It is therefore strange that filmmakers do not seem to realise this. At the end of most feature films the credits roll on interminably, and perhaps after the third tea-maker has been credited, a brief reference may be made to the locations used! Television films seldom go even that far. If the *Morse* series is typical, there is a simple explanation: no records were kept, few remember.

So, to satisfy public curiosity, a peculiar sideline of tourist guiding has developed, which could be called 'location detection'. This involves painstaking video analysis, hunting down those involved in the filming, supplementing local knowledge by visiting suspected locations, and coming to terms with the wiles and deceits of the producers.

In analysing *Morse*, it became clear that only a few locations were given their real names. The Martyrs' Memorial was one. Many sites were filmed in Oxford but given fictional names, such as the colleges. Others were filmed a long way from Oxford but given Oxford names, for example Wytham Woods was often named but never filmed. Others were not named, but implied to be in or near Oxford when they were not, as with Morse's flat and the police station. As a general rule, if a scene was not clearly in Oxford, then it was filmed elsewhere, probably in an arc west of London from Surrey to Hertfordshire, where the film crew did not need to stay away. Each series was based at a studio – Bray, Wembley, Elstree, Shepperton – and they only came to Oxford, when it was featured, for a few days of a five-week shoot. Not all scenes are covered in my section on 'Other locations' in each episode, but they will be in the same area as those that are listed. Whatever their status, they are all described as 'Locations'.

In his *Morse* novels, Colin Dexter could easily move his characters through the Oxford he knows so well. It was not so simple for the filmmakers, faced with crowded streets and reluctant shop owners. To their credit, they seldom fell back on studio sets or library footage. In time, the computer 'morphing' that, for example, transformed the dining hall of Christ Church into the almost unrecognisable Hogwarts hall of Harry Potter, may dispense with real places and even actors. The heyday of the 'location detectives', squeezed between the old-style studio sets and the computer whiz-kid, will soon be over.

The *Morse* novels were written by a Classics scholar and champion crossword compiler, who created a complex character partly in his own image. His plots, and the personalities, were much changed for television. It was a risk to expect viewers to stay with involved plots over two hours, and a 'star' was needed. John Thaw brought his own style and created a very different policeman to the one in the novels. The first trial series of three films in 1987 were adaptations of Dexter novels, but through to 1993 all but four of the twenty-three stories were original screenplays, and Oxford as a location receded, and in six episodes did not even appear. Trailed as the last episode to be made, *The Twilight of the Gods* returned vividly to the university.

The principle actors were now involved with other productions, and it became difficult to bring them together. Colin Dexter had written the prize-winning *The Way Through The Woods*, and the excellent annual episodes based on his new novels followed, culminating in the death of Morse in *The Remorseful Day* (2000). One exception was *The Wench is Dead*, previously overlooked from 1989, in which Kevin Whately could not appear.

Parts 3 and 4 of this guide may be of interest to both readers of the novels and TV viewers. To avoid confusion, Parts 1 and 2 describe only the TV films. Colin Dexter was heavily involved in the filming, advising on plots and making cameo appearances in most of the episodes. Even so, his novels, which inspired it all, are ignored here, and for this reason it is doubly generous of him to have contributed his Foreword. Other acknowledgements to all those who have helped are made at the back of this book, which I hope is a fitting testimonial to a much-loved series and a beautiful city.

Nuffield College.

Sheep Street, Burford.

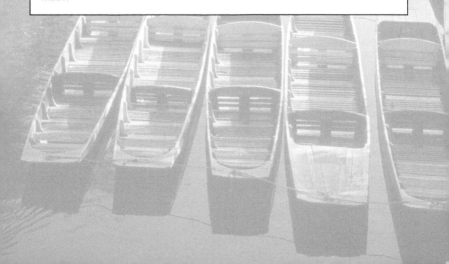

PART 1

FROM YOUR ARMCHAIR

In this part, all of the episodes with an Oxford setting are summarised, and known locations given. The events are not necessarily listed in chronological order. Readers unfamiliar with the stories, who wish to remain so before they view the films, may choose to ignore the plot summaries.

Up to the seventh series, made in 1992 and shown in early 1993, episodes were concurrently made, mainly in groups of four. Despite the resulting confusion, expert editing created groups of distinctive stories, each with a sense of 'place', and with plots that roughly made sense.

One Morse novel, *The Secret of Annex 3*, was never adapted, and another, *The Jewel That Was Ours*, was written after the film *The Wolvercote Tongue* was made.

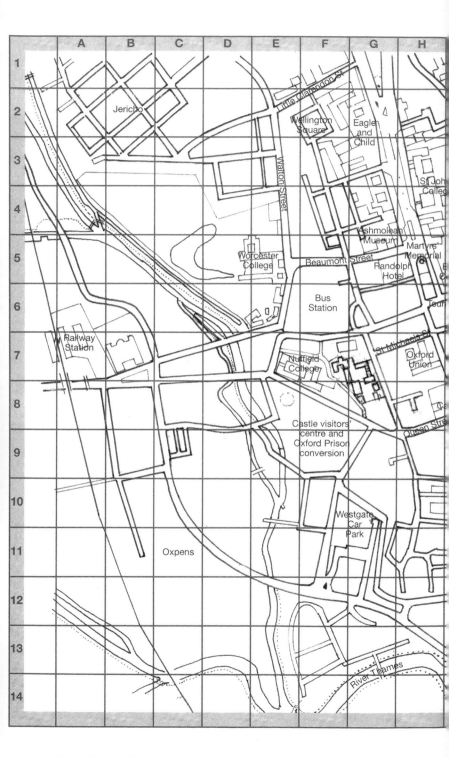

Map of Central Oxford.

1 THE DEAD OF JERICHO

SERIES 1	6TH JANUARY 1987
WRITER	ANTHONY MINGHELLA
DIRECTOR	ALISTAIR REID

BASED ON THE 5TH MORSE BOOK, PUBLISHED 1987
ALMOST 14M VIEWERS

SUMMARY

Minghella chose this, his favourite *Morse* novel, for the opening film. The adaptation was somewhat stylistically confused and disappointed Colin Dexter. However, opening and closing, 'Sweeney-style', with the beloved Jaguar being rammed, the action is full of wit and allusion. They are in Jericho, where George Jackson is repairing Anne Staveley's wall, and Morse improbably climbs a wall when Lewis catches him. Morse is a Singing Detective. Sophocles would be surprised to find himself prominent in a 20th-century police series! There is an Agatha Christie-style showdown with the suspects. PC (The Blue Lamp) Dixon represents old-style coppers. Patrick Troughton, an admired actor, asked for some redeeming virtue in his character of George Jackson, so they gave him a rabbit to stroke!

Morse is perplexed by all the first names of the conspiring Richards family beginning with A. The personalities of the main characters are established, Morse over-educated and erratic, Lewis the opposite.

John Thaw was already white-haired; nobody expected the series to last thirteen years. He is unlucky in love, perhaps this time due to that terrible leather jacket!

OXFORD LOCATIONS

The White Horse, Broad Street Morse and Anne Staveley have a drink after choir practice.

The Bodleian Library area: Clarendon Building, Sheldonian Quad, Radcliffe Square Morse accompanies Anne on the long route back to Jericho.

Mansfield Road also on the walk back to Jericho.

JERICHO AREA

Combe Road (Canal Reach) a short road of terraced cottages. Anne's cottage was last on the right. George Jackson lives opposite, from where he spies on Anne. Ned Murdoch is a lodger. The final showdown takes place here.

Old Bookbinders Ale House (then The Bookbinders Arms) Morse explains situation and theories to Lewis. The internal scenes, of a large bleak room, are elsewhere.

Old
Bookbinders
Ale House.

Canal Street.

Canal Street Morse detects a smell in the nearby telephone box, and thinks it fishy. The box is now removed.

Walton Street George cycles home after collecting blackmail money (although Ned wrote the demand), followed by Alan Richards.

Magdalen College Morse questions Ned, who attacks him and runs off. Morse has passed Colin Dexter in the cloisters, and gives him a backward glance.

Morse drives via **Longwall Street** to hear Tony Richards' talk on his turntable business, at which time Jackson is murdered in **Canal Reach** and a half-blinded Ned is admitted to hospital with a drug overdose.

Morse interviews Ned's tutor in the **cloisters**.

Gill & Co. Ltd, Wheatsheaf Passage Lewis checks on Anne's keys, and is told Morse has one.

Police Station, St Aldates Lewis drives Morse from the police station, up the **High Street**, into **Oriel Square** then into the **Radcliffe Infirmary**, to try to see Ned.

BACKGROUND VIEWS
Radcliffe Observatory, Tower of the Winds, Green College.
Hertford Bridge (Bridge of Sighs), Hertford College.
The Oxford University Press.

OUTSIDE OXFORD

Southall the garage where the Jaguar is rammed (now a supermarket).
Royal Holloway Sanatorium, Virginia Water the choir rehearsal room.
Dorney Common Jackson collects the blackmail money.
Bray Studios (back of) Alan and Adele Richards' house.

2   THE SILENT WORLD OF NICHOLAS QUINN

SERIES 1   13TH JANUARY 1987
WRITER   JULIAN MITCHELL
DIRECTOR   BRIAN PARKER

BASED ON THE 3RD BOOK, PUBLISHED 1977

SUMMARY

This is Colin Dexter's favourite adaptation of all his novels, perhaps because it touches on two areas close to him. It was increasing deafness that led to his retirement from an examination board, and to start writing in his retirement. Crosswords figure prominently. The plot is complicated, with Morse, after defeating the guilty people of the Town in *The Dead of Jericho*, taking on the academics of the Gown. There are clever people committing over-clever crimes – right up Morse's street, but compared to the baroque episode that followed, quite ordinary. Corrupt members of the Foreign Examination Syndicate murder Quinn, then Ogleby, to prevent discovery of malpractice, and attempt to frame the Director. Monica reprises Anne Staveley of the first episode as a typical Morse heroine, an English rose with passions running deep, but not for Morse, and Bartlett's disturbed son replicates Ned Murdoch. The embarrassment surrounding the notorious *Last Tango in Paris* sets the prurient mood of the time.

OXFORD LOCATIONS

St Mary the Virgin scene from the tower over **All Souls College** to Headington, where it is implied that the Syndicate Headquarters lies.

Brasenose College (called Lonsdale) Morse interviews Roope in his room in New Quad. Later Roope observes Lewis lurking in the quad, and leads him through Old and Chapel Quads and out into **Radcliffe Square**.

Exeter College Somehow Roope gets into the Fellows' Garden, emerging from a door into **Brasenose Lane**. Lewis runs into the square and ends up above him on **Exeter's Fellows' Garden** wall, looking down on a smirking Roope.

Lewis then emerges from **St Edmund Hall** gate into the **High Street**. Roope comes out of **The Magna Gallery**, glances at a disgusted Lewis and goes on to the **Botanic Garden** where, by a hothouse, he meets Dr Bartlett. Thus ended possibly the most inept trail in TV history!

Oriel College Front and St Mary's quadrangles. A reception is being given for the Sheik of Al-jamara in the **dining hall** by Oxford's Foreign Examination Syndicate which supervises O-level and A-level examinations for students abroad. Profoundly deaf Nicholas Quinn has a malfunctioning hearing aid and lip-reads a conversation across the room which appears to implicate Dr Bartlett

The Phoenix cinema
on Walton Street.

in the sale of secret exam papers. In the **Front Quadrangle** he tells Phillip
Ogleby of his suspicions, thus sealing both their fates. Morse walks with the
Dean through **St Mary's Quadrangle**.

JERICHO

Studio 2 cinema Walton Street, now **The Phoenix** Monica Height parks
   outside the University Press and sees Bartlett coming out of the cinema,
   showing *Last Tango in Paris*; she looks in former Cycle Shop (now Loch Fyne
   Restaurant) and when he has gone goes into the cinema. The ticket stub for the
   film becomes important in the plot, and later Morse and Lewis go to check on it.
The Railway Station Christopher Roope meets the Dean of Lonsdale College
   as they come off the train, establishing his alibi.
Merton Street Postmasters Hall disguised as The Horse and Trumpet pub,
   where Monica takes Morse.
The Jaguar is shown driving past the **Sheldonian** with its guarding heads, up
   Parks Road and stopping at **The Radcliffe Observatory**, where Ogleby's
   doctor is interviewed.
Radcliffe Infirmary Morse interviews Monica in hospital.
The Jericho Lewis drops Morse at the cinema to see *Last Tango in Paris*, only
   to see that *101 Dalmations* has replaced it. Lewis drives off to pick up his family,
   leaving a disappointed Morse to drown his sorrows in the pub.

OUTSIDE OXFORD

St John's Beaumont School Andrew Rex Windsor Examination Syndicate
   headquarters.
Boveney Court Dorney Nicholas Quinn's house.
High Street Windsor Ogilvy's house.
Royal Holloway Sanatorium the inquest court where Roope is arrested.
28 Castlebar Park, Ealing, West London Morse's flat.

3   THE SERVICE OF ALL THE DEAD

SERIES 1	20TH JANUARY 1987
WRITER	JULIAN MITCHELL
DIRECTOR	PETER HAMMOND

BASED ON THE 4TH BOOK, PUBLISHED 1979

SUMMARY

After the first two straightforward episodes this is a step into gothic horror, not to Morse's taste, although the devious plotting conspirators certainly are. A slightly untypical church group has conspired to kill Simon Pawlen, the blackmailer brother of their vicar, and pretend his body was the churchwarden Harry Josephs. Josephs then goes on a spree to kill the conspirators. Blackmail, theft, revenge, gambling and child abuse seem to be the motivations. This is the bloodiest episode of all the films, with six bodies, almost seven if Morse had not been twice rescued by Lewis, first from the falling Lionel Pawlen and then from Harry Josephs on the church tower. Morse has his first kiss, with Ruth Rawlinson. St Michael's provides an excellent tower for people to fall off, the views from it appreciated by Lewis but not Morse!

The episode is typical of Peter Hammond's style; full of reflections, glowing colours and interesting camera angles, and the quality of the 16mm film is fully exploited.

OXFORD LOCATIONS

Panoramic view over Oxford, down onto **St Michael's Church Bray**.
Blackwell's Bookshop Morse comes out into **Broad Street**, but as he plays his new tape he gets the call to go to St Oswald's. Morse drives by the **Clarendon Building** the graveyard of **St Mary Magdalen** (the church in the novel).
Radcliffe Infirmary summoned from the police station, Morse and Lewis visit Max, the Jaguar is left in an ambulance bay.
Broad Street Lewis calls on the manager of Lloyds Bank (where the Tourist Information Centre is now situated).
Merton College Morse discusses Lionel Pawlen with the Archdeacon, walks across Front Quad (passing Colin Dexter) into Mob Quad then to the chapel door.
The Turf Tavern after Ruth refuses a dinner date with Morse, he and Lewis go under **Hertford Bridge** to The Green Man, where he sees Ruth in conversation with a man. A disappointed Morse startles Lewis by leaving without having a beer, and without looking at the man, murderer Harry Josephs.

BACKGROUND VIEWS
All Souls College from the tower of St Mary the Virgin and reflected in Denmans' (solicitors) window.

The Turf Tavern.

New College Bell Tower from Turf Tavern.
Radcliffe Camera, Clarendon Building and **Tom Tower.**

OUTSIDE OXFORD

St Michael's Church, Bray near **Maidenhead** all the church scenes.
River Thames seen from the church tower and where Brenda Josephs' body
    found. **Bridge at Henley-on-Thames.**
Dorney Court near Windsor, Ruth Rawlinson's workplace.
Wimbledon Common Ruth Rawlinson's house.
The Trout Inn, Wolvercote pub scenes.
West London courtroom and police cell.

4   THE WOLVERCOTE TONGUE

Series 2	25th December 1988
Writer	Julian Mitchell
Director	Alistair Reid

Based on the book *The Jewel that was Ours*, published 1991

SUMMARY

Here a relatively straightforward story is sandwiched between the macabre horrors of *The Service of all the Dead* and *The Settling of the Sun*. The central theme of the disappearance of the Wolvercote Tongue, a Saxon artefact being returned to the museum by the Poindexters, ends relatively crimeless, with a simple insurance scam. This story strand shared characters with the real action, in which a jealous husband kills his wife's lover and then her. No one comes out of it too well, including city tour guides!

OXFORD LOCATIONS

St Giles in contrast to the peaceful opening view across **Port Meadow** to the Oxford skyline, the road is bustling with traffic including a coach carrying a group of American tourists. A frazzled courier, Sheila Williams, gives a brief history of the **Martyrs' Memorial**. Later Cedric Downes takes the Americans on a tour of Oxford and on the Memorial steps demonstrates how not to be a tourist guide, being corrected several times by Janet Roscoe. Later Downes takes the group into the garden of **New College**, where he forgets the reason the college was so named, giving Janet a chance to pounce again.

Randolph Hotel where the tourists stay, and one of them, Laura Poindexter, dies of a heart attack in Room 310. The Tongue is missing. Morse and Lewis discuss the case in the (now) Morse Bar. Dexter, writer Julian Mitchell and Brasenose College bursar Dr Robert Gasser sit in the background. Sheila introduces the group to museum direcor Theodore Kemp and Dr Cedric Downes in the lounge.

Eddie Poindexter and Shirley Brown walk down **Broad Street** with the **Clarendon Building** in the background.

Ashmolean Museum Sheila meets Kemp outside. He tells her that their affair is over. Morse and Kemp cross to the museum to view the jewel-less buckle. Morse discusses Mrs Kemp's suicide with Sheila Williams in the sculpture gallery.

The Railway Station Lewis trails Howard Brown to the station, then to the **Didcot Railway Centre**, where Morse joins him. Later Brown sees Poindexter and a young woman on a train. The detectives drive via the **University Parks and Woodstock Road** to interview Downes at the station. Morse drives them past **Nuffield College** to **The Trout Inn**, where Poindexter explains on the terrace that he had thrown the Tongue into the river for the insurance, at which

The Randolph Hotel.

point a frogman recovers the jewel. Morse and Lewis stand on the terrace and the weir bridge.

OUTSIDE OXFORD

The Trout Inn, Godstow Morse and Lewis stand on Godstow Bridge looking at the floodlit pub. Later, the Tongue is recovered from the River Thames by a police diver.

Newark Priory, River Wey, Ripley, Surrey Kemp's naked body tumbles over a small weir and beaches, to the horror of a picnicking couple. Called the River Cherwell in the episode. Also fiming at the River Colne, Uxbridge.

Didcot Railway Centre Morse and Lewis interview steam engine enthusiast Howard Brown.

Church art Ealing West London Poindexter meets his daughter.

Paddington Station Lucy Downes is murdered in a telephone box. Morse suspects correctly that she was carrying Kemp's clothes.

5   LAST SEEN WEARING

Series 2	8th March 1988
Writer	Thomas Ellice
Director	Edward Bennett

Based on the 2nd book, published 1977

SUMMARY

Following the macabre third and fourth episodes, and preceding the grotesque sixth, this is a quiet, almost victimless story, but the seediness of the book on which it was based pervades the scenes. The central plot involving the disappearance of a schoolgirl is flimsy, not helped by Morse forging a letter from her, and failing to recognise her beneath a superficial disguise. The death of Cheryl Baines may even be an accident. Morse is morose throughout and seems unwilling to believe that it was Lewis who betrayed him to an aggressive Strange. Far more dramatic events await our heroes.

OXFORD LOCATIONS

Magdalen Bridge and College, Museum of the History of Science, Sheldonian Theatre The serenity of the opening scenes, and the music, contrasts with the noise of building work outside Morse's window. The name on the machine, Craven, will become familiar.

The White Horse Morse and Lewis are too late for service.

Christ Church Library Morse speaks to Sheila Phillipson, the headmaster's wife. They walk into **Oriel Square**, she towering above Morse, despite the fact that Lewis identifies her from her small stature, the cycle and the anorak.

OUTSIDE OXFORD

Reading Blue Coats School, Sonning Homewood School for Girls where Morse and Lewis interview Valerie's classmates.

St John Bapitise School Reading Acum's school.

Chelsea Harbour show flat and Maguire's flat.

Ex-Territorial Base, Harrow the police station.

Craven and Phillipson's houses Sonning – Reading area.

28 Castlebar Park, Ealing Morse's flat.

6   THE SETTLING OF THE SUN

SERIES 2	15TH MARCH 1988
WRITER	CHARLES WOOD
DIRECTOR	PETER HAMMOND

SUMMARY

Following his macabre *The Service of All the Dead* and the imaginative *The Wolvercote Tongue*, director Peter Hammond directs another melodrama, the body count in his three episodes totalling a creditable fifteen. Throughout, the director's trademark is the use of glass and reflections. This was the first film not based on a Dexter book.

The plot unfolds at Brasenose College, a crucial element being the duious theory that only the Japanese can tell each other apart, but then if Morse had looked at the bodies he might have solved the case quicker! Confused relationships, revenge, unlikely connections and death abound. It is Yukio Li, the drug dealer, who 'did it' before being croqueted by a mallet wielded by Mrs Warbut. Robert Stephens, as the Master Sir Wilfred, gets the chance to play the first of the corrupt college heads in the series. Unlike four later heads, he survives. Even college servants have a chance to be sinister. If the series is to be sold in Japan, this episode might be left until last!

OXFORD LOCATIONS

Bodleian Library Old Schools Quadrangle a pensive Morse comes past the statue of the 3rd Earl of Pembroke, across the Quadrangle and out of the main gate, holding an exhibition programme entitled 'Images of Christ Giotto Dali' that shows the stigmata.

Oriel College the dining hall in the early scene.

Exeter College chapel and Front Quadrangle a tearful wheelchair-bound Reverend Robson looks at his damaged palm, watched by his daughter Jane. Later, Mrs Warbut comes out of the chapel as Morse goes in. He then chases an intruder, unavailingly of course, into Palmers Tower, the former college gatehouse.

At the end Mrs Warbut, after killing Yukio Li, flees to the chapel and on the altar explains her revenge. Morse continues to moralise as she collapses, then arrests her. He joins Sir Wilfred in Exeter's Front Quad, then meets Alex, Jane's niece.

Magdalen Bridge Morse and Jane Robson, the current object of Morse's affection, push her wheelchair-bound father over the bridge and then, presumably finding they had gone too far, retrace their steps.

Botanic Garden in a hothouse the Reverend Robson rises nimbly from his wheelchair and attacks a gardener wearing an unlikely hat.

Radcliffe Square a coach arrives, viewed from the tower of **St Mary the Virgin**, with members of a summer school, and they enter Lonsdale College to be greeted by the Japanese-speaking-and-hating domestic bursar Mrs Warbut.

Brasenose College (called Lonsdale) a reception dinner is interrupted by the discovery of a dead Japanese, assumed by Morse, who was at the dinner, to be Yukio Li. Morse's reflection talks to Lewis while Max examines the body. As usual Morse prefers not to look at the corpse, gazing out of the window at the pinnacles of the **Old Schools Quad**. Morse addresses the group in the hall, goes through the college gymnasium with a disturbed Jane to look for records. They emerge in Brasenose New Quad before arriving at the Bursary. Jane and Morse talk in **Brasenose New Quad.**

The Turf Tavern Morse and Lewis chat, including about poetry.

Radcliffe Infirmary where Jane recovers and is visited by Morse.

OUTSIDE OXFORD

Hunting Lodge Hotel, Monkey Island, Dorney Reach, Berkshire Jane plays croquet.

Guildhall Yard, City of London (now redeveloped) Gentlemen's W.C. where the body of Graham Daniel is found. Max puts his finger on a slight weakness in Morse's technique; 'thought why there wasn't more (blood) or were you just grateful?' Morse 'I was grateful'.

7   THE LAST BUS TO WOODSTOCK

SERIES 2	22ND MARCH 1988
WRITER	MICHAEL WILCOX
DIRECTOR	PETER DUFFELL

BASED ON THE 1ST BOOK, PUBLISHED 1975

SUMMARY

This episode was based on the first Morse book, inspired by Colin Dexter seeing a blonde at a bus stop on the Woodstock Road one dark rainy night, although in Dexter's case a young man. The blonde of the story, Sylvia Kane, accepts a lift and dies in the car park of a Woodstock pub, the Fox and Castle. Giving the lift is a Dr Crowther, whose girlfriend, thinking Sylvia is a rival, attacks her. As she lies unconscious she is accidentally run over by Crowther's car. The detectives investigate muddled relationships at her workplace, but this is aepisode where not too much happens. It also assumes that good-looking young women are likely to fight for the attention of an elderly married male academic, so it would have been popular in the Senior Common Rooms and with mature men everywhere! It is also the last episode for pathologist Max, played by the distinguished actor Peter Woodthorpe, who wanted a larger part in future stories.

OXFORD LOCATIONS

Opening rainy scene from **Pembroke Square** to **Tom Tower** of **Christ Church.**

Worcester College student Angie Hartman enters the college, and speaks to Dr Bernard Crowther and Peter Newlove in the Front Quad. Peter watches as Angie delivers her essay to Crowther.

Gill & Co. Sanders works at Gill's and when sacked, smashes up display goods.

Hertford College Morse attends Crowther's lecture on Rochester. Colin Dexter is in the audience.

Scenes in **St Giles, Radcliffe Square, Keble College**.

OUTSIDE OXFORD

Windsor End, Old Beaconsfield, called Woodstock Road.

Effingham Junction Station, near Leatherhead, Surrey site of the Fox & Castle, where Sylvia Kay dies in the car park.

Grove Park Hotel Burnham Bucks.

Between Maidenhead and Cookham wood where Crowther and his wife dump the incriminating tyre.

8 THE GHOST IN THE MACHINE

SERIES 3	4TH JANUARY 1989
WRITER	MICHAEL WILCOX
DIRECTOR	PETER DUFFELL

SUMMARY

This is an episode right back on form, and the second one not based on a Dexter novel. At its heart is a typical Morse heroine, her icy exterior covering smouldering passion. Patricia Hodge is just right as a gardener-friendly aristocrat, although for once not the object of Morse's desire. Most of the action takes place at the country house where his neglected wife kills Sir Julian Hanbury. She and her lover then throw the body off the roof, and then bludgeon it to make it appear the work of an intruder, which would allow an insurance claim. This plot would have fooled your average detective (and viewer)! There is a sub-plot with a blackmailing au pair and boyfriend killed in an unlikely car crash. Enter Dr Russell to replace Max and create sexual tension.

OXFORD LOCATIONS

Oriel College opens with Fellows of Courtenay College meeting to discuss candidates for Master, tied between Professor Ullman and Hanbury. Later Morse interviews Ullman and there is a rare opportunity to see an Oxford tutorial being given.

Oriel Square Ullman arrives at the college.

The Railway Station Lady Hanbury arrives, as does Morse, and gives Betty Parker a lift.

OUTSIDE OXFORD

Wrotham Park, Hertfordshire Hanbury Hall for the house and domestic scenes.

Nuneham Courtenay, Oxfordshire, chapel and gardens Ullman visits, argues with Hanbury. Later Hanbury's body is found in the chapel.

9 THE LAST ENEMY

SERIES 3   11TH JANUARY 1989
WRITER   PETER BUCKMAN
DIRECTOR   JAMES SCOTT

BASED ON THE BOOK *THE RIDDLE OF THE THIRD MILE*, PUBLISHED 1983

SUMMARY

Morse comes up against his favourite criminals: devious, murdering, philandering and vengeful academics. It starts with a mutilated body in the Oxford Canal, followed by an attempted garroting in London. A woman student, Deborah Burns, is sleeping with Sir Alexander Reece, the head of her college, and believes that he has betrayed her. Clues on the canal body lead Morse to the college where old rivalries with Reece surface. Morse tramples happily over Whitehall and the area of the Metropolitan Police. Professor Drysdale murders civil servant and Honorary Fellow Nicholas Ballarat and dumps him in the canal. Reece murders Professor Kerridge, Drysdale shoots Reece – it turns out to be an everyday story of university folk! Morse has toothache.

OXFORD LOCATIONS

Carfax Morse, on the way to Beaumont College, walks across, discarding a local newspaper.

Corpus Christi College (called Beaumont) Morse walks across the croquet lawn. He then walks along the cloisters with Carol Sharp. They then emerge in **Brasenose** back quad. Reece is shot in his college room, Deborah flees. Morse and Lewis walk in the cloisters.

Brasenose College (also called Beaumont) Morse and Carol go into the Buttery. Lewis calls to get college scandal from Kerridge's scout.

Radcliffe Square/Catte Street Morse and Lewis walk along Catte Street and across the Schools Quadrangle.

Sheldonian Quad Morse expresses his suspicion to Lewis that Reece is murdering his way to becoming head of the university, Lewis is unconvinced.

Turl Street Walters Outfitters; Lewis checks on the suit on the canal body, then meets Dr Russell and helps her choose a present.

Radcliffe Infirmary Dr Russell and Morse find a common love of fountain pens.

Cornmarket Professor Drysdale is chased before colliding with bicycles.

Nuffield Hospital Drysdale's room.

OUTSIDE OXFORD

Oxford Canal, Thrupp basin the story opens with a decapitated dismembered body found in the canal. The detectives go to The Boat pub (**The Jolly Boatman**) to interview the landlord. Lewis visits Kerridge's cottage. Morse and Lewis return to canal, a boatman indicates that the missing head would probably have been washed upstream! Lewis assists young lady to cast off. The detectives again visit The Boat.

3 Horseshoes, Winkwell pub scenes.

LONDON

Southall TA Centre Police Station.

Camden Arts Centre the picture gallery where Morse and Reese talk about Kerridge.

Brunel University the pathology laboratory.

Hillingdon Hospital the autopsy room.

Pall Mall club where Kerridge meets Chris Stonely.

28 Castlebar Park, Ealing Morse's flat.

Paddington Station Morse arrives in London.

Archery Tavern, Bathurst Place W2 Morse meets Reece's student Deborah sitting alone in a pub. Morse, in Lewis's absence, has to buy her a drink!

Bayswater, Cleveland Square, W2 Kerridge is attacked (by Drysdale) and later killed by Reece.

Piccadilly Circus, Admiralty Arch en-route to Whitehall.

St James' Park Morse and Lewis walk after visiting Ballarat's **Whitehall** department. **Buckingham Palace** is in the background.

Regents Park, London Zoo Morse questions Deborah.

Reggae Club West London.

10 DECEIVED BY FLIGHT

SERIES 3	18TH JANUARY 1989
WRITER	ANTHONY MINGHELLA
DIRECTOR	ANTHONY SIMMONS

SUMMARY

The plot is primarily about the export of illegal drugs using the cover of a college old boys' cricket team, The Clarets. In a sub-plot an adulterous wife kills an old student friend of Morse. Lewis poses as the college porter and while he is playing for The Clarets, a customs investigator on the trail of the smugglers is killed in the pavilion. Morse somehow deduces that the drugs, on the way to Europe, are concealed in a wheelchair, not that customs officers would have thought of that! He also works out that his old friend Anthony Donn had intended to murder his adulterous wife but that she had got her retaliation in first. The body count of five is inflated by early scenes of three victims of an arson attack on a bookshop, where sparks fly with Dr Russell. This is Kevin Whateley's favourite episode, as he likes cricket and the ground was near his home, and more than any other shows the father-and-son-style relationship between Morse and Lewis that is crucial to the series.

Pembroke College Quadrangle.

OXFORD LOCATIONS

Botanic Garden Morse and Anthony Donn eat fish and chips, talk about Zen and one-hand clapping, **Magdalen Bridge** is in the background.

Pembroke College here Donn is found electrocuted, and Lewis acts as a porter and replaces Donn in The Clarets cricket team. Kate Donn with Morse meets Roland Marshall and Vince Cranston in the back quadrangle; Morse is remembered as being called Pagan. Lewis is observed following customs officer Foster, whose view across open countryside from his college room is *not* from Pembroke!

Oriel and Hertford Colleges various internal scenes.

OUTSIDE OXFORD

St Annes Road, Holland Park, West London the arsoned bookshop, now a private house.

Mill Hill School (cricket ground) Lewis tracks Foster to a cricket pavilion; as usual his trailing ends in disaster, this time by getting his head batted. During the cricket match Foster is stabbed in the pavilion. The evil Cranston commits one of the worst crimes in the series by running out Lewis, as well as dropping a catch off his bowling!

Beaconsfield Station the railway station.

Kate Donn's radio studio BFBS Paddington.

Denham Bucks the Donn's house.

Danesfield House Foster's apartment (now an hotel).

Dover ferry port as The Clarets leave, Morse observes Kate Donn and Cranston in close conversation. Drugs are found in Marshall's wheelchair.

11 THE SECRET OF BAY 5B

SERIES 3   25TH JANUARY 1989
WRITER   ALMA CULLEN
DIRECTOR   JIM GODDARD

SUMMARY

Gowned criminals are resting; this is the town's turn for mayhem, revolving around building contract corruption, a scheming wife, and manipulation of car park tickets to establish alibis, suicide and murder. Mel Martin's wife seems adequate reason for the men to slay each other! Lewis gets his head banged again. We say goodbye to Dr Russell, who was getting too close to Morse!

OXFORD LOCATIONS

Magdalen Bridge George Henderson throws a cassette into the River Cherwell.

The King's Arms where Rosemary Henderson sits, and where later Morse and Lewis meet.

Lime or New Walk Morse and Lewis walk down towards the River Thames from Christ Church.

Magna Gallery, High Street Brian Pierce takes paintings to sell.

The White Horse where Morse meets Dr Russell and leaves her to pursue architects' receptionist Janice into **Broad Street**.

Westgate Multi-storey car park, St Ebbes Morse approaches, **Tom Tower** of **Christ Church** in the background. The body of architect Michael Gifford is in a car; Morse gets unusually close to it.

University Boat House (now burnt down) and across the Thames the new college boat houses on Codgers Island. Edward Manley is arrested during a simulation of the 'Eights' rowing regatta.

OUTSIDE OXFORD

Porchester Hall, Porchester Road, Bayswater Morse and Dr Russell dance a terrible quick step. Morse is fortunately called away by Lewis.

Shepperton Studios (called the Westgate Multi-storey car park)

Sefton Park, West London the insurance office.

Highgate North London The architects' office where Lewis is coshed.

The Dewdrop Restaurant Gifford parks outside a fictional restaurant named after Colin Dexter's local pub.

Harrow Leisure Centre the squash game and aerobics class.

Woods near Caversham, Berks (called Wytham Woods) where George Henderson works. Lewis opens a barrier, a cowled jogger passes by, and the detectives startle Rosemary in Henderson's shed.

Wytham village and White Hart pub Rosemary goes into a phone box.
Holland Park Camilla's and Janice's flat.
Summertown library Rosemary leaves Morse's car keys outside.

12 THE INFERNAL SERPENT

SERIES 4   3RD JANUARY 1990
WRITER   ALMA CULLEN
DIRECTOR   JOHN MADDEN

THIS WAS THE FIRST SCREENPLAY NOT BASED ON A PLOTLINE BY COLIN DEXTER.

SUMMARY

Yet again a college head is portrayed in an unflattering light, this time that he has a past of child abuse. A number of people are out for revenge, but it is his wife that finally gets him, to the frustration of the gardener, who has already tried unsuccessfully. Furthermore the college is involved with Corbi-International, a corrupt chemical company. The early scenes concern an attack on Dr Dear, on his way to address an environmental debate.

Freed from Oxford-loving Colin Dexter for the first time, it appears that the writer and director decided to portray Oxford in a poorer light even than usual, and their parody of the head of a college has angered Merton College, whose head is actually a distinguished woman academic.

OXFORD LOCATIONS

Without obvious reason the cameras roamed confusingly between three adjoining colleges.

Merton College (called Beaufort) Patey's and Front Quadrangles. In a downpour (water cannons) the Master of Beaufort College, Matthew Copley-Barnes, and Dr Julian Dear leave the college for the Oxford Union debate. The Master goes back for papers, giving Dear his umbrella. The professor is attacked. The Master, following on, is barged against a wall, and the attacker runs into Beaufort.

At a family party in the Fellows' Garden, a parcel arrives for the Master containing a horned animal skull.

Sylvie Maxton arrives in the Front Quad. Jake Normington conducts a choir. Morse and Lewis wander on the croquet lawn. Morse talks about music and Dear with Normington.

Morse pursues Mick McGovern, Normington's friend, identified as Dear's assailant by the porter. Normington packs to leave.

Phil Hopkirk, the gardener, frustrated at having mistakenly attacked Dear due to confusion over umbrellas, and being beaten to the Master by his wife, smashes up flower planters in the Front Quad.

Morse finds Sylvie in his lodgings with the Master's battered body. The Junior Common Room in the Front Quad was converted to make the lodge.

Morse quotes Milton's *Paradise Lost* as he leaves the college.

Ship Street McGovern is helped over a wall in the rain. As he was trying to get

Merton College Fellows' Garden.

into Merton College it would presumably have been a surprise to find himself in **Jesus College. Exeter College** is in the background.

Oriel College Dear's funeral service held in Oriel's chapel after mourners enter **Merton** dining hall. Lunch is taken in the dining hall.

Oriel Square the Master's wife talks to Phil Hopkirk about his daughter.

Oxford Union Morse arrives at the Oxford Union for the debate that environmental issues transcend party politics. Dear's death cancels it.

University College Chapel the Master's wife looks at the Van Ling windows with images of the serpent. Imogen and Morse find her. She is persuaded by Morse not to jump off the organ loft, and is escorted out of Merton's dining hall!

Radcliffe Infirmary Morse finds a man with McGovern's mother, gives chase unavailingly.

Randolph Hotel Sylvie moves into the hotel and meets Morse. Morse leaves the hotel for the Master's lodgings.

EPISODES 13, 14, 15, 16, 20, 23 AND 25

In the middle of the series, free of the influence of Colin Dexter (see Foreword), several episodes were made mainly away from Oxford. The locations of these are summarised below.

13 *The Sins of the Fathers* Brakespeare's Brewery, Henley-on-Thames; McMullen & Sons Brewery, Hertford; Ye Old Fighting Cocks (pub), St Albans; and Worcester College library. The Trout Inn, Wolvercote.

14 *Driven to Distraction* Crowthorne Vehicle Test Centre, Berkshire; Vauxhall garage, Radlett, Herts; The Kent pub, Pitshanger Lane, Ealing; Headington Hill.

15 *Masonic Mysteries* Chiswick Town Hall; St Albans Cathedral and Close; The Royal Oak (pub), Kitter's Green, Herts; 28 Castlebar Park, Ealing W5 (as Morse's flat).

16 *Second Time Around* in Oxford The Eagle and Child (as Shears Wine Bar), Radcliffe Infirmary, Randolph Hotel, The Railway Station and The Trout Inn, Wolvercote. Outside Oxford Luton Hoo, Bedfordshire; Shenley Lodge, Herts.

20 *Promised Land* in Australia Sydney and the Sydney Opera House; Canowindra and Cowra, New South Wales.

23 *The Death of the Self* in Italy Vicenza and Verona; in the UK Harefield, Hertfordshire.

25 *Cherubim and Seraphim* Mentmore Park, Bedfordshire; Ye Old Greene Manne (pub), Batchworth Heath, Hertfordshire; Harmsworth Park House, Feltham, West London.

17 FAT CHANCE

SERIES 5	27TH FEBRUARY 1991
WRITER	ALMA CULLEN
DIRECTOR	ROY BATTERSBY

SUMMARY

This episode adds virulent misogyny to the various sins of male college Fellows. One of the women Fellows, preparing to stand for the position of college chaplain, is poisoned by an unidentified substance which is identified as a slimming chemical, taken accidentally. There is a sub-plot of a dubious slimming organisation 'Think Thin', aided by a corrupt chemist, opposed by the women, but no murders. Morse for once seems to get some satisfaction, before the usual unhappy ending.

OXFORD LOCATIONS

New College (St Saviour's) in the chapel, a group of women take Holy Communion, then walk across the Front Quad. One of them, Dr Victoria Hazlett, wearing a BA gown and with her arm in a sling, goes in for a further examination but collapses. Hilary Dobson finds her room ransacked, and later says that the women's movements records have been taken. Morse and chaplain Lance Mandeville walk in the cloisters and into the ante-chapel by Epstein's statue of Lazarus, and into the chapel where Morse looks closely at El Greco's painting of St James. He learns of antipathy towards the women's group. Geoffrey Boyd has pictures of women clerics on walls of his room.

The women clerics arrive for the election of the college chaplain; Hilary Dobson does a cartwheel on the lawn of the Front Quadrangle after winning. Morse finds Emma had neglected her chaperone duties.

The Jaguar is driven down **High Street**, up **Queen's Lane** and stops in **New College Lane**, before entering **New College** summer entry.

Nuffield College Hilary and Emma Pickford sit on the Upper Quad lawn. Emma meets Morse, they walk into the Lower Quad, she accepts a dinner date; later his flowers appear to have been a good investment.

The Railway Station Lewis and Dobson find the missing tampered bicycle.

OUTSIDE OXFORD

Heathmount School, Hertfordshire (The Think Thin Club) the missing Dinah Newberry runs wild as candidates for slimmer of the year parade.

18   WHO KILLED HARRY FIELD?

SERIES 5	13TH MARCH 1991
WRITER	GEOFFREY CASE
DIRECTOR	COLIN GREGG

SUMMARY

Another eponymous hero, like Nicholas Quinn, makes an early, brief and fatal appearance. A rich art collector, Paul Eirl, has employed Harry Field's father to forge masterpieces. Harry also paints forgeries and cleans pictures, and has threatened to expose the fraud, following a dispute over Eirl's interest in Harry's regular model, Jane Marriott. Presumably unaware that Harry's motorcycle is at a pub close to his estate, Paul kills him and takes the body some miles away. Field senior probably then kills Eirl in revenge. A sub-plot has Lewis wanting promotion.

Colin Dexter was once more involved with the script, and translated the spoof genealogy, which amused Morse, into Latin. The film is visually rich, a rare treat for art lovers, the style set by the original Morse production designer David McHenry, and original paintings by Meg Surrey. Pheloung's music is also prominent in this episode.

Wadham College.

OXFORD LOCATIONS

Broad Street Morse parks before going into Blackwells.

Blackwell's Bookshop Morse talks to Helen Field.

Holywell Music Room Morse consults Ian Matthews about the forged Whistler, and later about Dürer's picture of Giovanni Bellini.

Christ Church Picture Gallery Morse and Lewis talk to Harry Field's father. **Peckwater and Tom Quads** Morse meets Lewis outside Christ Church library, they then walk into Tom Quad.

The Victoria Arms on the lawn, Lewis asks Morse to recommend him as an inspector, Morse replies, reluctantly, that he would. Ornamental students are punting in the background.

Wadham College Morse meets Matthews in the Front Quad, also in the group is Colin Dexter.

The Railway Station Helen meets Harry's father. Morse leaves for London.

Museum of Modern Art (now Modern Art) Morse visits the gallery.

Pembroke Square and College Lewis trails Tony Doyle inconclusively.

OUTSIDE OXFORD

The Trout Inn, Wolvercote Morse takes Helen Field for drinks.

Brocket Hall, Lemsford, Herts Paul Eirl's mansion. Now an exclusive hotel, stunningly filmed.

Nicholas Hawksmoor Upper School, Borehamwood Tony Doyle's school.

Royal College of Arms, London Morse's visit leads him to Paul Eirl.

The Crooked Chimney pub, Lemsford, Herts the motorcycle is found.

Shenley Hospital, Herts the water tower in Harry Field's picture.

Keatings Way Harry's road (a visual joke on Tom Keating's famous art forger).

19 GREEKS BEARING GIFTS

SERIES 5	20TH MARCH 1991
WRITER	PETER NICHOLS
DIRECTOR	ADRIAN SHERGOLD

SUMMARY

Back with the academics, and it was all Greek to Morse for most of the episode! A college Fellow, Randall Rees, is an expert in Greek triremes, his wife Friday a TV presenter. On a visit to Greece he fathers a child, and the mother and boyfriend with eponymous baby come to Oxford, probably with blackmail in mind. The boyfriend is killed, the baby kidnapped, the Greek girl killed in the same way with a broken neck. Friday Rees did it, but Rees, who is clearly a loser, is arrested after Friday dies in a fall. A Greek tycoon takes an unlikely close interest in a small restaurant, giving Morse an opportunity to be rude to his financial superiors. Mrs Lewis makes a first appearance.

Covered Market.

OXFORD LOCATIONS

Magdalen College Morse enters the floodlit college. At dinner he meets Greek specialist Randall Rees and his wife. There is a scene in the library with Jerome.

Oxford Union students at a lecture in the Debating Chamber humiliate Rees. Morse watches, then interviews him and later talks to friend Jerome about Anglo-Greek relations at the time when the trireme film was made.

Ship Street Rees walks with shopping.

Covered Market the dead boyfriend's sister, Maria, escapes from interpreter Jocasta. Jocasta runs out of the **Golden Cross Yard**, Maria is phoning in **Carfax**.

Greek Taverna, Summertown (implied) the Greek restaurant.

Note: the name Friday is an abbreviation of Frideswide, Oxford's patron saint.

OUTSIDE OXFORD

Southwark, London Morse interviews the shady Digby Tuckerman.

Highwood Park House, Barnet, Hertfordshire Tuckerman's house.

Heathrow Airport Tuckerman meets Maria.

Greece on film.

River Wey, Ripley Surrey (called the Cherwell) angler pulls up the hand of Maria.

Huntercombe Manor, near Maidenhead, Berks final scene where Friday holds the child over a stairwell.

21   DEAD ON TIME

SERIES 6   26TH FEBRUARY 1992
WRITER   DANIEL BOYLE
DIRECTOR   JOHN MADDEN

SUMMARY

This is a painful episode for Morse. He cannot believe that his old love Susan Fallon conspired with her fatally ill husband and a doctor to frame the man who had been responsible for the death of their daughter and grandchild. Lewis has to investigate on his own. There is confusion with the timing of telephone calls. Lewis destroys the tape that incriminated the old flame after her suicide, stoically withstanding Morse's derision of his 'solution'.

OXFORD LOCATIONS

Sheldonian Theatre Morse takes Susan to a concert after her husband's death.
Sheldonian Quadrangle/Clarendon Building scenes around the concert.
Hertford College there is a drinks party on the front lawn after the concert.
Magdalen College, Holywell Mill Stream, Addisons Walk Morse and Susan talk on the bridge over Holywell Mill Stream, and again in the water meadows. Lewis finds Morse after Susan's suicide; they go around Addison's Walk. Lewis throws the tape incriminating Susan into the **River Cherwell**.

OUTSIDE OXFORD

Senate House, University of London Susan's university.
Nether Winchendon House, Bucks William Bryce-Morgan's house.
Bloomsbury London the inquest court.
St Michael's Church Bray interview with Helen Marriat.
Harrow TA Centre Police Station.

22 HAPPY FAMILIES

SERIES 6   11TH MARCH 1992
WRITER   DANIEL BOYLE
DIRECTOR   JOHN MADDEN

SUMMARY

There is mayhem at the Balcombe family estate, with sub-plots of antagonism between Morse and the press, and a police fête. Margaret Cliff is responsible for three Balcombe deaths, Jessica for another, and counting the earlier murder of Steven Ford by the Balcombes, there is a body-count of five.

OXFORD LOCATIONS

New College Morse consults friend Josh about the family. Reporters talk mockingly about Morse at the Garden Quad gate.
Carfax Colin Dexter appears as a drunk.
Exeter College and **The Mitre** (pub) appear in the background.

OUTSIDE OXFORD

Shirburn Castle, Watlington, Oxon the Balcombe family home.

New College garden gate.

24   ABSOLUTE CONVICTION

SERIES 6	8TH APRIL 1992
WRITER	JOHN BROWN
DIRECTOR	ANTONIA BIRD

SUMMARY

This is a lightweight story packed with heavyweight actors. Three fraudsters are in an open prison; their financial advisor is outside keeping their money warm. One prisoner dies, another is attacked and another prisoner, Charlie Bennett, whose wife was killed by the advisor who then framed him, gets his revenge. There is a good foot and car chase through Oxford.

OXFORD LOCATIONS

Oriel Square Morse and Lewis drive through **Oriel Square**, see prisoner Charlie Bennett sitting on a wall. Lewis gives chase while Morse drives, Bennett goes up **Blue Boar Lane**, dodges through **The Bear**, up **Wheatsheaf Passage** and across the **High Street** into the **Covered Market**. The chase ends with Morse falling over a greengrocery stall. Bennett, actually out of prison on parole, helps him up. They drink tea in **Browns Café**.

New College Lane/Queens Lane Lewis picks up Morse.

Radcliffe Square/Catte Street Morse talks to prison governor Mrs Stevens after she comes out of the **Schools Quad.**

OUTSIDE OXFORD

HM Prison, Grendon Underwood, Bucks the prison.

Eton College chapel Morse sings in a choir, Barrington Pheloung conducts; Mrs Stevens watches and later talks to Morse in the cloisters.

Rossway Park, Herts (Cryer's mansion)

The Greyhound (pub), **Aldbury, Herts** usual pub talk.

The Bear.

26 DEADLY SLUMBER

Series 7	8th January 1993
Writer	Daniel Boyle
Director	Stuart Orme

SUMMARY

Businessman Michael Steppings, working with vengeful nurse Wendy Hazlitt, sets up a false alibi, and then murders surgeon Dr Brewster who bungled his daughter's minor operation. He then blackmails son John Brewster to falsely confess to protect his family's reputation, but is killed by John.

OXFORD LOCATIONS

The King's Arms John Brewster's girlfriend Jane Folley follows him from the Kings Arms into Catte Street; tries to persuade him to come out.

Christ Church Morse calls to see John in the library. Colin Dexter shows them into the library; his first speaking part: 'Mr Brewster'.

Oriel College Morse talks to Jane Folley, walks through to two back quads. Later John removes aqualung equipment from a locker, talks to Jane in college.

Oriel Square Morse intercepts Jane; she discloses that her breathing equipment is faulty and could not have been used in John's father's murder.

Magpie Lane Morse and Lewis discuss the case, and later walk from **Turl Street** into **Broad Street**.

River Thames at a boathouse by Donnington Bridge, incriminating evidence is found in Jane's locker.

Worcester College library Library scene.

Radcliffe Infirmary Lewis establishes that Mrs Brewster was too ill to commit murder and that she was not the anaesthetist on the day of Steppings' daughter's operation.

88 St Aldates Morse calls on nurse Wendy Hazlitt, discuss suspect Michael Steppings, who is later identified as having sent threatening letters to dead surgeon. Later Morse sees her painting of Steppings' garden, establishing their connection. He waits in St Aldates.

Science area, Parks Road the new pathologist is consulted.

OUTSIDE OXFORD

Water Mill, Chenies, Bucks Steppings' house.

The Black Swan, Martyrs' Green, Cobham, Surrey Steppings' alibi is partly established.

27 THE DAY OF THE DEVIL

SERIES 7	13TH JANUARY 1993
WRITER	DANIEL BOYLE
DIRECTOR	STEPHEN WHITTAKER

SUMMARY

Psychopath serial rapist John Peter Barrie, assisted by the prison psychiatrist, escapes and goes after old accomplices whilst also becoming involved in a devil-worshipping cult centred on an Oxford college. Bizarre rituals in woods, disguises and revenge all add to the interesting reputation of Oxford's academics!

OXFORD LOCATIONS

Balliol College one of the university's most illustrious colleges has its bursar, Maugham Willowbank, portrayed as an occultist. There are various scenes with bursar and odd-job man Steven Trevors.

High Street Andrews estate agents, to check on recently rented property.

OUTSIDE OXFORD

Between Maidenhead and Cookham wood where black mass ends in ring of fire and murder.

Eton High Street the bookshop.

Princes Risborough occult goods shop.

28 TWILIGHT OF THE GODS

SERIES 7   20TH JANUARY 1993
WRITER   JULIAN MITCHELL
DIRECTOR   HERBERT WISE

SUMMARY

Philanthropist Andrew Baydon, due to be honoured by the university, gets Grimshaw, his bodyguard, to shoot a reporter investigating his past war crimes. In the Encaenia (honourary degree) ceremony, Morse's heroine, Welsh diva Gwladys Probert, is shot. It takes Morse a long time to work out the shot was not meant for her. A war-victim has tried to shoot Baydon, so that his trial would expose the crimes. Full of vivid Oxford scenes, and with Sir John Gielgud as the Chancellor displaying nicely expressed insensitivity (he thought the Proctors should be investigating), and Robert Hardy matching him as the evil Baydon, who describes Morse as 'that superannuated policeman with that scrap heap of a car' (hard but true, the car was almost impossible to drive!). 19 million viewers watched this episode, trailed as the last.

OXFORD LOCATIONS

Holywell Music Room Morse attends a master class given by Gwladys. Behind him is Susan McCulloch, the actual singer, listening to her own voice. At the end, a pensive Morse drives past the Music Room and into Broad Street.

Sheldonian Theatre with the Modern History Faculty in the background. The diva's effete hairdresser is told to sit down, the Chancellor wants his lunch.

Sheldonian Quadrangle/Clarendon Building the Encaenia procession passes down Broad Street and the Clarendon Building. Mari Probert is on her mobile, an early use of this device. Baydon and Gwladys walk side by side; Glwadys is shot. Lewis clears the quad. Superintendent Strange arrives. Morse interviews the Vice-Chancellor and talks to Strange and Baydon; Welsh text is read. Baydon, who has said the shot was more likely for him, nevertheless wanders around the cleared quadrangle with Morse, who tries to establish a link with Grimshaw.

Magdalen College Arabella Baydon talks to the boyfriend in the cloister; finds her room ransacked and a crucial airmail letter stolen.

Radcliffe Square/Catte Street there is an aerial shot of the central university area from Andrew Baydon's helicopter. Baydon talks to reporters outside Brasenose College gate. Baydon leaves in a hurry; his helicopter drowns out the Chancellor's speech. Victor Ignotas is found in the Modern History faculty library.

Brasenose College the Chancellor (John Gielgud) rehearses his speech, talking about other Oxfords.

Christ Church Mari Probert and her boyfriend walk on the Broad Walk in the Meadows. The post-ceremony party gathers in Tom Quad, but lunch is in Trinity College. The picture behind the Chancellor is of Mary I.

Oriel College Gielgud is at his insulting best in the dining hall.

Bodleian Library Reading Rooms Morse and Lewis go through the strangely unevacuated reading rooms seeking to find from where the shot came. A revolver is found behind books.

John Radcliffe Hospital (JR2) Morse, then Mari, visit Gwladys. Lewis sneaks out to the Jaguar. Morse realises at last that the shot was intended for Baydon, and talks with Arabella about her brother Fred.

OUTSIDE OXFORD

Newark Priory, River Wey, Ripley, Surrey (Morse calls it The Isis, slang for the Thames). Neville Grimshaw's body is discovered in a punt.

Englefield House, Charlton Woodville, Near Reading Baydon's House. Lewis interviews Madam's hair stylist and has his first proposition!

Denham Village and pub village scenes.

29 THE WAY THROUGH THE WOODS

THE SPECIALS	16TH NOVEMBER 1995
WRITER	RUSSELL LEWIS
DIRECTOR	JOHN MADDEN

BASED ON THE 10TH BOOK, PUBLISHED 1992

SUMMARY

Karen Anderson, with a past criminal record, kills Dr Myton, an attempted rapist; George Daley, a blackmailer; her husband David Michaels, who had helped fake her death by marrying her; and almost Lewis, in the woods. A photographic group for whom she erotically modelled included a college bursar, Dr Alan Hardinge, but he was only a mild pornographer and adulterer, really quite normal. Lots of policemen argue! Dr Laura Hobson arrives with a nice line in put-downs directed at Morse.

OXFORD LOCATIONS

Oxford Prison prisoner Parnell is attacked and denies murdering Karen Andersen, before expiring. The chaplain tells this to Lewis who tells Morse, confirming Morse's doubts that Parnell murdered Andersen.

Exeter College (named Lonsdale, normally the pseudonym of Brasenose College). There is a drinks party on top of Fellows' Garden wall, below which the Jaguar drives through **Radcliffe Square** and up **Brasenose Lane**. Morse attends a concert in the garden and flirts with Claire Osbourne, and later revisits

Fellows' Garden, Exeter College.

the college and meets Dr Alan Hardinge, the bursar. Harding makes a phone call. Morse searches Daley's shed in Exeter College.

Turl Street Morse visits Titles bookshop (now Past Times), meets Claire again, and borrows a book on Pre-Raphaelites and Millais. He returns the book and gets a date.

Police Station Lewis leaves as Morse arrives. Morse is criticised by Strange and taken off the case. Johnson assaults Phillip Daley, to Lewis's dismay.

Park Town Hardinge calls on osteopath McBryde; later Morse and Lewis visit and trap McBryde into admitting he and James Myton photographed Karen. The trail leads to Hardinge and, due to the Millais postcard, to Wytham Woods.

Morse calls at the **University Land Registry** to enquire about access to **Wytham Woods**, where he intuitively feels Karen lies. Meets David Michaels.

The Eagle and Child (pub) where Morse patronises and angers Lewis.

OUTSIDE OXFORD

Blenheim Palace and Park Daley's body is found. Pathologist Dr Hobson enters. Morse interviews Williams in Blenheim Park. The Grand Bridge can be seen in the background.

Leith Hill, Dorking, Surrey, the wood and forester's cottage in the opening scene a dog disturbs a skull. Morse drives to Michaels' cottage, meets Cathy Michaels (aka Karen Andersen and Kate Burns); again Morse is uncomprehendingly face-to-face with a missing girl, as in *Last Seen Wearing*.

A police search in the woods finds the skeleton of Myton, not Karen as expected.

In the final scene in woods, Cathy Michaels shoots David Michaels and gets Lewis to dig his own grave. Somehow Morse arrives and Cathy is shot.

30   THE DAUGHTERS OF CAIN

THE SPECIALS   27TH NOVEMBER 1995
WRITER   JULIAN MITCHELL
DIRECTOR   HERBERT WISE

BASED ON THE 11TH BOOK, PUBLISHED 1994

SUMMARY

Terminally ill teacher Julia Stevens organises with other women the death of the husband of one of them, Ted Brooks. He was a former Wolsey College drug dealer and the murderer of Felix McClure, a college Fellow who covered up his dealing. Pupil Kevin Costyn is seduced into assisting. There is subtle use of the weapon, a Rhodesian knife, stolen by Brooks, now a museum attendant, from the Pitt Rivers Museum cabinet. A heart attack prevents him from returning it and it falls into the hands of 'the Daughters'. They get Kevin to break into the cabinet to make it look as if the knife was stolen *after* they had killed Brooks! Mrs Stevens outsmarts the detectives, to Morse's admiration and Lewis's disillusionment.

OXFORD LOCATIONS

Wadham College reception on the Front Quad lawn, dinner in the hall (this is founder-writer Julian Mitchell's old college).

University Museum/Pitt Rivers Museum the Jaguar drives up to St Giles; Morse goes to the University Museum then through into the Pitt Rivers Museum. Lewis discusses the missing Rhodesian knife with a Pitt Rivers curator. Pupil Kevin, recruited by the women, steals a knife from a cabinet in the Pitt Rivers while they go on a trip to Stratford. Morse correctly solves the riddle of the knife.

Knives at the Pitt Rivers Museum, with the dagger in the centre.

CARLTON UK PRODUCTIONS LTD
INSPECTOR MORSE: "THE DAUGHTERS OF CAIN."
Production Office: Building 35 Shepperton Studios, Studios Road, Shepperton, Middlesex TW17 OQD
TEL (01932) 562611   FAX: (01932) 569918
Direct Tel to Prod Office: 01932 572029   Direct Fax to Prod Office: 01932 572488

CALL SHEET NO: 15

PRODUCER: CHRIS BURT
DIRECTOR: HERBIE WISE

LOCATION: Christchurch College
SETS 1 - 4:   St Aldates Street
   Oxford
Contact::   Mr Richard Benthall
Tel: 01865 276178
   (As per movement order no 17)

PRODUCTION OFFICE:
TRINITY ROOM
OXFORD MOAT HOUSE
DIRECT TEL: 01865 316890 and 01865 316891
DIRECT FAX: 01865 316892

DATE: Friday August 30 1996
UNIT CALL: 08.00   At Location
UNIT M'BUSES: 07.15   Leave Hotel
BREAKFAST AVAILABLE FROM: 07.15

UNIT BASE: Oxpens Coach & Lorry Park
   Oxpens Road
   Oxford
Contact   Bob Peedell
Tel: 01865 794307

Sunrise: 06.10
Sunset: 19.51
Mobiles: Jerry: 0585 776412
   Dennis: 0831 490602
   Simon: 0850 527663

	SETS:	SCENE NOS:	D/N	PAGES
1)	EXT. WOLSEY COLLEGE - QUAD	23.	DAY	1 3/8
2)	EXT. WOLSEY COLLEGE - DRINKWATER QUAD	51.	DAY	1 6/8
3)	INT. WOLSEY COLLEGE - PRESIDENT'S LODGINGS	131.	DAY	3/8
4)	INT. WOLSEY COLLEGE - PRESIDENT'S LODGINGS	37.	DAY	1 4/8

ARTISTE	CHARACTER	P/UP	MAKE-UP/ WARDROBE	L/UP ON SET
SETS 1-4 EXT/INT. WOLSEY COLLEGE Scs: 23. 51. 131. 37.		**DAY**		
JOHN THAW	MORSE	07.15	07.30	08.15
KEVIN WHATELY	LEWIS	08.15	08.30 at unit base	
BENJAMIN WHITROW	BROWNLEE	06.45	07.00	08.00
ANGELA CATHERALL	MRS BARNETT	06.45	07.00	08.00
EXTRA ARTISTS:				
1 Man	College Don		07.00	08.00
Mixed	College Students		07.00	08.00
Mixed	Visitors		07.30	08.00
1 Man	Custodian (Continuity Sc: 53)		07.30	08.00
1 Man	Tourist (Continuity Sc: 53)		07.30	08.00

PROPS: As per script and art dept instructions to include: Envelope, snapshots of Kay
   with McClure, snapshots of Kay, Rodway and Davies, various pictures of Kay

ART DEPT: College flag at half mast - Sc: 23

ELECTRICAL: Small wind machine

STAND-INS:	**FOR**	**ON SET**
Barry Summerford	Mr Thaw	08.00
Julie Brown	Utility	08.00
George Higgins	Utility	08.00

CAMERA: As per Nigel Slatter's instructions

SOUND: As per Bruce White's instructions

ELECTRICAL: As arranged with Colin Powton

Call sheet, *The Daughters of Cain.*

The Oxford University Museum of Natural History.

Christ Church (Wolsey College) Morse discusses fund-raising and McClure's death in Tom Quad with Dr Brownlee; goes through McClure's room.

Oriel Square Morse and Brownlee in Oriel Square look at photo of Kay Brooks and McClure, walk into Christ Church. Morse asks Lewis to see Ashley Davies at racing stables on the Berkshire Downs.

Radcliffe Square/Catte Street Ted Brooks' bicycle, stained with McClure's blood, is found where he left it after his heart attack.

River Thames Brooks' body is found by a college boatman in an inlet of the Thames by **Donnington Bridge**. There are more good lines for Dr Hobson when Morse shies away from the corpse. The boatman says the body would have been washed upstream! The missing knife is extracted from Brooks' body.

The Railway Station Morse meets Kay Bach, and then takes her for a drink.

The Victoria Arms, Marston where they have a drink, and a punt trip on the **River Cherwell**; naturally a boatman awaits!

OUTSIDE OXFORD

Opens with aerial shot over **Keble College**, then **Harefield Hospital, London**, from out of which comes Mrs Stevens.

Lambourne racehorse gallops, Berkshire Downs Lewis sees Davies, Kay's fiancée.

The Crown, Bray, Berks Morse suspects Davies.

Top: The Trout Inn.
Above: The Morse Bar at the Randolph Hotel.

Opposite above: Weir from terrace of the Trout Inn, Wolvercote.
Opposite below: Morse and Lewis.

31 DEATH IS NOW MY NEIGHBOUR

THE SPECIALS   1ST NOVEMBER 1997
WRITER   JULIAN MITCHELL
DIRECTOR   CHARLES BEESON

BASED ON THE 12TH BOOK, PUBLISHED 1997

SUMMARY

Rivalry for a college headship leads to Angela Storrs, the ambitious wife of a contender, mistakenly shooting the neighbour of a blackmailing reporter (because there is no 13 Bloxham Drive), and then the reporter Geoffrey Owens. Daughter Diane provides an alibi for Angela at a hotel in Bath but her breakfast choice gives her away. Meanwhile the other ambitious wife, Shelly Cornford, gives herself to the outgoing vengeful Master Sir Clixby Bream. Her husband is ungratefully enraged. Morse meets Adele Cecil, admits to the Christian name Endeavour.

OXFORD LOCATIONS

Oriel College Cornford discusses power play in Oriel second quad. Academics walk across Oriel Front Quad. Shelly Cornford falls down stairs as Morse and Lewis pass by. The service is in the chapel; dining is in the hall (Dexter says Latin grace).

Brasenose College other college scenes.

Aerial shot from **Carfax tower**. Morse and Lewis drive down the **High Street** to see Owens' body.

The offices of *The Oxford Times*, Osney Mead where reporter Geoffrey Owens works.

Le Petit Blanc, Walton Street, Jericho Geoffrey Owens lunches with a girlfriend.

Radcliffe Square/Catte Street Denis Cornford gets out of his car in Radcliffe Square, runs through **Brasenose College gatehouse** and into **Oriel College** for meeting on successor to Sir Clixby Bream, who does not want to be succeeded, either by Cornford or by Julian Storrs. Morse and Lewis discuss the case in floodlit Radcliffe Square, where later Morse has to refuse an invitation from Dr Hobson.

Little Clarendon Street Denis Cornford buys his wife a dress for the college feast.

Botanic Garden/Magdalen Bridge Morse and Adele drive under **Hertford Bridge** (Bridge of Sighs) and down **New College Lane**, then walk over white bridges crossing the **River Cherwell** in **Magdalen School grounds**.

OUTSIDE OXFORD

Weston Turbville, Bucks the site of Bloxham Drive.

The Crown, Bray, Berks Morse and Lewis discuss the case.

The Royal Crescent Hotel, Bath Circus, Bath the Storrs stay to establish Angela's alibi; after seeing the breakfast menu Morse realises it was really the daughter who was at the hotel and not her mother.

Marston village church Church scene.

Above: Hertford Bridge
and New College Lane.
Right: Radcliffe
Observatory.

Opposite above: The
Sheldonian Theatre.
Opposite below: Radcliffe
Square and Camera.

32 THE WENCH IS DEAD

THE SPECIALS 11TH NOVEMBER 1998
WRITER MALCOLM BRADBURY
DIRECTOR ROBERT KNIGHTS

BASED ON THE 8TH BOOK, PUBLISHED 1989

SUMMARY

Morse is still seeing Adele Cecil but is in deteriorating health and talking about retirement. He is investigating a period in which the canals were in similar health, railways making inroads into their commercial trade and passengers having better options.

In hospital, goaded by American historian Dr Van Buren, Morse attempts to prove that the 1859 Oxford Canal murderers were wrongly convicted. With assistance from Kershaw, not from Lewis, who is on an inspector's course, he deduces that the boatmen of the flyboat *Barbara Bray* had been wrongly convicted of the murder of passenger Joanna Franks. He establishes the motive to be an insurance claim devised by Joanna's husband, Charles Franks, otherwise known as illusionist. From shoes and clothing found in the Record Office he deduces that the victim was taller than Joanna. The deception is confirmed by the opening of her coffin, in Ireland, which contains only rocks. Morse totally undermines Van Buren's hardback book; it was unwise of her to give him the chance! There are great Victorian scenes, atmospheric Pheloung music, and the only trial scene in the whole series.

OXFORD LOCATIONS

Bodleian Library/Divinity School Dr Van Buren walks across Schools Quad and into the Library, where in a reading room she is served by Dr Robert Gasser (whose voice was dubbed, being thought too deep for a librarian's!) and sees Kershaw researching for Morse. They then walk into The Grove of Trinity College from **Parks Road**.

Old Courtroom, Town Hall trial of the boatmen.

Oxford Prison hanging of boatmen.

St John's Street/Wellington Square dept of Criminology, part of the University Law School where evidence of the Canal case is held. (**Kellogg College** is in the background.)

Science area, School of Pathology Dr Hobson analyses the old evidence.

Randolph Hotel Adele talks to Strange about Morse's retirement and asks for assistance in the investigation.

The Railway Station Morse sees off a still-unconvinced Dr Van Buren, and then meets Adele.

Wadham College Van Buren speaks to Morse from her room. They walk from the Front Quadrangle into South Parks Road.

Oxford
Canal boat
station and
St Barnabas'
Church.

St Sepulcre's
cemetery.

Dukes' Cut, Oxford Canal, near Wolvercote (called Princes Cut) where
police arrest the boatmen.

St Sepulcre's Cemetery, Jericho almost certainly where the murder victim
would have been buried.

OUTSIDE OXFORD

St Peter's Hospital, Chertsey (implied JR2 Oxford) Morse ill, Strange makes an
inflammatory visit. Dr Millicent Van Buren gives him a copy of her book on the
Oxford Canal Murders 1859. Morse leaves at the end after medical clearance.

Black Country Museum, Dudley Joanna Franks embarks on the barge.

Braunston Marina, Oxford and Grand Union Canals. The opening scene on
the canal.

The Barge Inn, Pewsey, Wiltshire (Kennet Canal) Morse and Kershaw
drink.

Castlebar Park, Ealing, West London Morse's flat.

Bertnaghboy Bay, west Ireland Morse and Adele find the empty coffin
confirming Morse's theory.

Lyceum Theatre, London Donovan's act.

Above: Punts on the River Cherwell, Botanic Garden.

Opposite top: Magdalen Bridge.
Opposite middle: Bridges over the River Cherwell in Magdalen College school ground.
Opposite below: A self-propelling punt!

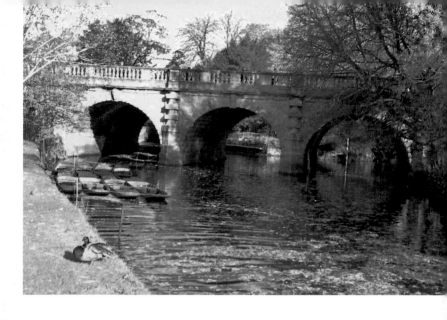

33 THE REMORSEFUL DAY

THE SPECIALS	15TH NOVEMBER 2000
WRITER	STEPHEN CHURCHETT
DIRECTOR	JOHN MADDEN

BASED ON THE 13TH BOOK, PUBLISHED 1999

SUMMARY

From the outset it is clear that this is unlikely to be a cheerful finale. An ill Morse receives a sad letter from Adele in Australia. There is a flashback to mayhem in a country house, starting with jealous daughter, Dr Sandra Harrison, killing her mother Yvonne. Strange, having realised that Morse was involved with Yvonne, had taken him off the case.

The murder had led to blackmail by three locals, but they fell out, and one, the shared lover of mother and daughter, murdered the other two. He in turn is killed by Simon Harrison, who like Nicholas Quinn in episode 2 and also Paddy Flynn, is deaf and lip-reads, a theme of personal interest to Colin Dexter. Another failed trail by Lewis, as he loses Harry Repp. Morse is ill but interferes in the case and although he and Lewis argue, the phlegmatic Lewis does not sulk. Medical professor Sir Lionel Phelps is a nasty and lecherous, but for once an innocent, academic. Adele dumps Morse from Australia. Morse collapses in Exeter Quad from a heart attack, and dies in hospital, having with his last gasp solved four murders. Lewis arrests Sandra at Heathrow.

Colin Dexter considers the last chapter of his novel The Remorseful Day *to be the finest piece of writing of his literary career. In it he gives the details of Morse's will, in which a third of his estate, about £50,000, is left to Lewis, a reasonable compensation for all the drinks he had bought.*

OXFORD LOCATIONS

Broad Street Simon Harrison works in Thorntons bookshop (now 'The Buttery'). Morse interviews, then arrests him after the anorak is recovered.

Randolph Hotel the scheming Harrison family dine in the restaurant. Morse questions Sandra, then Simon, about bird watching.

Exeter College Morse listens to Phelps singing Fauré's *Requiem* with a choir conducted by Pheloung in the chapel. Afterwards he walks with Phelps in the Front Quad, who discloses the Harrison link with Roy. Morse collapses on lawn of Front Quad as *In Paradisum* is played, and later dies in hospital after realising that it was Sandra's crutch that killed her mother! Sandra admits all, as all good Morse villains do.

Save the Children shop, High Street the incriminating tracksuit is dumped outside. The manager rings the police and identifies the driver who left it.

Production Office	PRODUCER: Chris Burt	Cell Phones on Set
Carlton Productions Ltd	DIRECTOR: Jack Gold	Alan Pinniger-Loc Man-0467 617659
" The Remorseful Day"		Charles Thompson-Ass Loc-0777 5654339
Shepperton Studios, Studios Rd		Ben Burt-2nd AD-0410 538044
Shepperton,Middx TW17 OQD		
Tel: 01932 572331		
Fax: 01932 572569	CARLTON PRODUCTIONS LTD	
	"THE REMORSEFUL DAY"	
Weather: Broken Cloud but dry		S'Rise: 06.27 S'Set: 19.41
Temp: 11-12'C		Shoot Day 26 of 28

PRODUCTION NOTE:

DATE: Thursday 6th April 2000	CALLSHEET # 26	CREW CALL: 08.00
		Line-Up: N/A

Location 1: St Peter's Hospital, Chertsey, Surrey	Unitbase 1: Homewood Park, Stone Hill Rd, Foxhills

Loc	SET/DESCRIPTION	SC #	D/N	PGES	CAST	B'GROUND
1	Int Radcliffe Hospital/Coronary Care-*Strange sends Lewis off*	158 if not shot	N8	4/8	2,3	B
1	Int Radcliffe Hospital/Corridor-*Sandra goes into her office*	21	D2	1/8	5	B
1	Int Radcliffe Hospital/Sandra's Office-*Sandra answers the phone*	22	D2	2/8	5	I
1	Int Radcliffe Hospital/Sandra's Office-*Sandra is leaving*	136	D8	2 pgs	1,5	I
1	Int Radcliffe Hospital/Corridor-*Sandra slaps Phelps for being suggestive*	61	E4	1 1/8	5,7	B
1	Int Radcliffe Hospital/Mortuary-*Lewis says goodbye to Morse*	167	N8	3/8	1,2,3	A
			Total	4 3/8		

#	ARTISTE	Status	Character	D/RM	P/UP	M-UP/ HAIR	W'DRB	L-UP	ON SET
1	John Thaw	W	Morse	Tr 1	09.30	10.30	10.15	N/A	11.00
2	Kevin Whately	W	Lewis	Tr 1	05.45	07.30	07.15	N/A	08.00
3	James Grout	W	Strange	Pos 1	07.00	07.30	07.15	N/A	08.00
5	Anna Wilson Jones	W	Sandra Harrison	Pos 2	07.00	08.00	08.45	N/A	09.00
7	T.P. McKenna	W	Prof Sir Lionel Phelps	Pos 3	11.30	14.00	As Ava	N/A	As req

Stand-in/Utility	Call	Background/Doubles	Call	M-up/Wdrb	On Set	Notes
David Adams or Kevin Whately	08.00	1x Mortuary Assis'	A	13.00 As Req	As req 07.00	Casting via Casting Collective
Barry Sommerford	08.00	10x Patients	B	07.00	As req	020 8962 0099
For John Thaw		3x Hospital Staff	B	07.00	07.00 As req	
Louise Cassie for Utility	08.00	4x Nurses	B	07.00	07.00 As req	

Requirements

Props/Art Dept:	Newspaper, vending cup/coffee sc 21,22. Boxes/belongings sc 136. White mortuary sheet sc167.
Computer:	Computer & keyboard + Techician c/o compuhire s/by 08.00
Medical:	Lucy Groghier, Medical Advisor on set today.
Camera:	As per Chris O' Dell
Grip:	Pneumatic wheels reqd.
Electrical:	As Per Vince Goddard
Sound:	As Per Brian Simmonds
Make-up/Hair:	As Per Maureen Hetherington
Wardrobe:	1x add' wardrobe assistant: Philipe Goldsworthy
Publicity:	Peter Mares, Tony Nutley on set today.
Rushes:	Sound Rushes to rtn' to Front Desk, Shepperton, Picture Rushes to go to Metrocolor on wrap.
Production:	1x add' Floor runner: Lucy Allen s/by 06.30, Julie Taylor from Kodak on set today.Mrs Allen + Daughter On set today.
Facilities:	1x Winniebago c/o Laurie Winter,1x Trailer, 1 x 3 Position, 1x M-up bus, 1xWardrobe bus, 2xDining Bus,1x crowd changing. 1xHoney Wagon Up & Running for 06.30, thankyou .c/o Filmscope.Tel: 01753 66258.
Catering:	07.15 B'fast. 13.00 lunch, 16.00 a'noon tea for 95 c/o Busters tel:077757 12491.

Call sheet, *The Remorseful Day.*

Gloucester Green Bus Station bus arrival.

Magdalen College Morse stands on terrace below **Magdalen Bridge**, tour guide thinks him part of her group, until he rudely rebuffs her.

The Railway Station Frank Harrison catches a taxi. Morse meets Lewis after Lewis had interviewed Frank; they then go to the charity shop to collect the red anorak, which is traced to Simon Harrison.

The Victoria Arms, Marston Morse and Lewis discuss the case, Morse quotes Houseman. Unusually in the series this is a wintry scene, in fact late March.

River Thames, Lower Wolvercote taxi driver witness, Paddy Flynn, is found dead in a car boot.

Top: Corpus Christi and Merton colleges.
Above: College bumping races on the River Thames.

Opposite above: Gowns.
Opposite below: All Souls College.

The *Morse* series ends with a misty view of the dreaming spires of Oxford taken from **Headington Hill South Park** to the east.

OUTSIDE OXFORD

33 Sheep Street, Burford philandering builder John Barron is knocked off his ladder by a jogger in a red anorak.

St Peter's Hospital, Chertsey Sandra Harrison is propositioned by Sir Lionel Phelps. Morse returns to the hospital to confront Sandra, who says she is going to Vancouver. Morse dies.

St Hubert's Home Farm, Gerrards Cross, Bucks Harrison's house, where his wife is trussed and dead on the bed. As a nurse she had tended Morse in hospital.

HM Prison, Bullingdon, Arncott, Oxon release of Repp.

Bicester and Oxford Bus Stations Lewis loses Harry Repp between Bicester and Oxford, thus completing a series of incompetent trails throughout the series.

The Queen's Head, Little Marlow, Buckinghamshire.

Castlebar, Ealing, West London Morse's flat.

Finchley TA Centre police HQ.

Wapsey Wood landfill site, Gerrards Cross, Bucks body of Harry Repp found.

Heathrow Airport Lewis arrests Sandra Harrison.

The Old Bakery and village, Denham, Bucks various village scenes.

St Mary the Virgin, Fawley, Bucks all the suspects attend Barron's funeral.

Exeter College chapel.   Sheep Street, Burford.

SOME FAVOURITE EPISODES

THE AUTHOR'S CHOICE

Twilight of the Gods Series 7 episode 28

This episode has everything, vivid scenes, drama, and great views of Oxford. Founder-writer Julian Mitchell has cunningly represented the worst characteristics of both Town and Gown. The 'Town', or non-university, represented by Baydon, craves recognition and adulation. The Gown is prepared to sacrifice its principles for money. There is a reminder that at one time the university administered its own laws. The detectives move with bemusement between the two sides. The script inspired bravura performances from John Gielgud and Robert Hardy, and hilarious support from the diva's fawning assistants, notably the stylist Allan Corduner and the gay voice coach Harry Ditson, whose scene with Lewis is a comedy classic. The luminous beauty of future Hollywood star Rachel Weisz is a bonus.

Trailed as the last Morse, 19m viewers in the UK watched it. Fortunately there were five episodes to come, although not for another three years. Otherwise this would have been a great finale.

The Wench is Dead The Specials episode 32

Colin Dexter's 1989 novel was passed over until 1998, but star writer Malcolm Bradbury shows what we had been missing. This is an atmospheric film with superb production values and music, and quite unlike any other in the series. Morse is ill, but for the first time in a happy relationship with a suitable companion, Adele Cecil. We see the crude policing of the 19th century, the intuitive detection of Morse, and get a glimpse of the bureaucratic finance-driven future abhorred by Strange and Morse. The villainous Charles Franks would not have prevailed if Morse had been around!

The Way Through the Woods The Specials episode 29

It is not quite clear why Morse is so convinced that the victim is in Wytham Woods, but in the end, fortunately for him, he is vindicated about the site, if not by much else. Meanwhile he has to endure much hostility, most woundingly from Lewis. This is a complex story of detection and well-drawn complex characters with a grand climax.

CAST'S AND CREATOR'S CHOICES

John Thaw *Masonic Mysteries*
Kevin Whately *Deceived by Flight*
Colin Dexter *The Silent World of Nicholas Quinn*

Top: Entrance to Merton College chapel.
Above: Christ Church library with Tom Tower in the background.
Left: Christ Church Gate to Oriel Square.

Opposite: 'Gown' students enter the Examination School.

PART 2

ON THE GROUND

The locations listed in Part 1 are rearranged in the form of a number of short walks, which can be linked together to suit various starting points and the time available. There are also sections on the Oxford waterways, and notable county locations.

Within Oxford, the routes include a mixture of civic and university sites. Part 3 gives the usual times colleges are open to the public, as a rule in the afternoon. Between the Morse sites are many notable buildings, a wide variety of high-quality domestic architecture and traditional pubs. Therefore each walk may take between 30 minutes and a full day to complete.

Armed with this book, you may choose to take a Morse tour from the Tourist Information Centre in Broad Street, Saturdays 1.30 p.m., and you will be able to correct your guide (which may be the author!) whenever a mistake is made, in the style of Mrs Janet Roscoe in *The Wolvercote Tongue*!

BEAUMONT STREET (WEST TO EAST)
ST GILES (SOUTH TO NORTH)

The most memorable scenes were set around the Randolph Hotel, opposite which are the Ashmoleon Museum and the Martyrs' Memorial.

Ashmolean Museum 4 The Wolvercote Tongue, *Theodore Kemp rejects Sheila Williams*
Worcester College 7 The Last Bus to Woodstock   13 The Sins of the Fathers 26 Deadly Slumber
St John Street 4 The Wolvercote Tongue

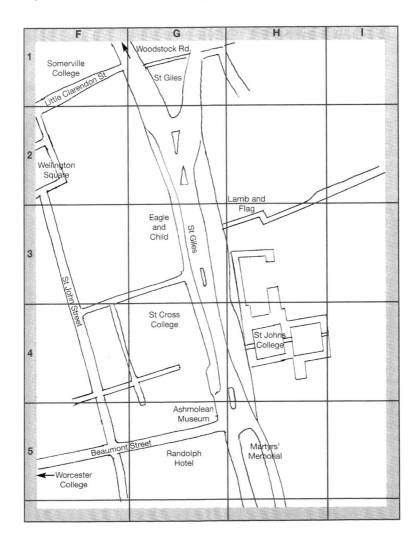

Above: Broad Street.

Opposite above: The High Street from St Mary the Virgin Church.
Opposite middle: Thrupp Canal Basin.
Opposite below: Cornmarket.

Randolph Hotel 4 The Wolvercote Tongue *the American tour party arrive and Laura Poindexter dies* 12 The Infernal Serpent 16 Second Time Around 32 The Wench is Dead *Adele Cecil pleads with Strange to give an assistant to the bedridden Morse* 33 The Remorseful Day *the scheming Harrison family take dinner*

Martyrs' Memorial 4 The Wolvercote Tongue *Cedric Downes makes mistakes in his talk to the tour party* 26 Deadly Slumber

St Mary Magdalen Graveyard (implied) 3 The Service of All the Dead

St Giles 4 The Wolvercote Tongue: *the tour party coach drives down. In several episodes the Jaguar is driven through.*

St John's College Morse's college in the book *The Riddle of the 3rd Mile*

The Eagle and Child (pub) 16 Second Time Around 29 Way Through the Woods

Woodstock Road 7 Last Bus to Woodstock *(implied, filmed at Old Beaconsfield)*

Radcliffe Infirmary 3 The Service of All the Dead

Green College 2 The Silent World of Nicholas Quinn

Woodstock Road 7 The Last Bus to Woodstock

Little Clarendon Street 31 Death is Now My Neighbour

Wellington Square 32 The Wench is Dead

BROAD STREET AREA (WEST TO EAST)

This area is rich in memorable filming locations and plot settings, the most notable being Exeter College and three Morse pubs.

Broad Street 3 The Service of All the Dead   4 The Wolvercote Tongue 11 The Secret of Bay 5B   26 Deadly Slumber   28 Twilight of the Gods   33 The Remorseful Day

Balliol College 27 The Day of the Devil

Thorntons Bookshop (now The Buttery) 33 The Remorseful Day

Tourist Information Centre (was Lloyds Bank) 3 The Service of All the Dead

Trinity College 9 The Last Enemy   32 The Wench is Dead *Dr Van Buren and DC Kershaw walk in the garden*   28 Twilight of the Gods

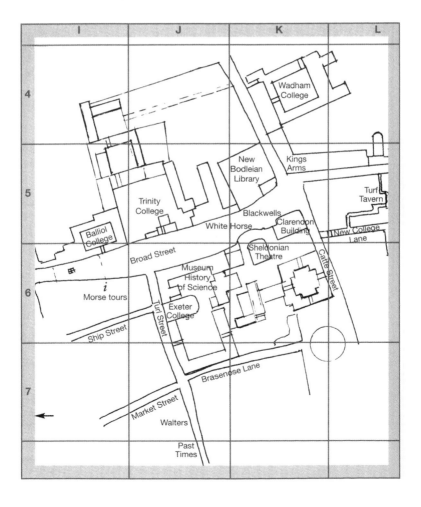

Top: New College Front Quadrangle.
Above: Christ Church College Front Quadrangle.

Opposite above: Morse.
Opposite below: University College chapel.

Turl Street 26 Deadly Slumber

Exeter College 2 The Silent World of Nicholas Quinn *Lewis chases Dr Roope in the Fellows' Garden* 6 The Settling of the Sun *Mrs Warbut lies on the altar in the chapel* 22 Happy Families 29 Way Through the Woods *Morse attends an open-air concert, intercut by a scene in which a skull is unearthed by a dog in Wytham Woods* 33 The Remorseful Day *Morse collapses in the Front Quad as a choir sings in the chapel*

Ship Street 12 The Infernal Serpent *Mick McGovern is helped over a wall in the rain* 19 Greeks Bearing Gifts *Randall Rees walks down*

Walters (outfitters shop) 9 The Last Enemy *Lewis calling to identify a suit, meets Dr Russell outside*

Past Times (called Titles bookshop) 29 The Way Through the Woods

White Horse 1 The Dead of Jericho *Morse drinks with Anne Staveley* 4 The Wolvercote Tongue 11 The Secret of Bay 5B *Morse runs out after Janice, leaving Dr Russell*

Blackwell's 18 Who Killed Harry Field? *Morse interviews Mrs Field* 3 The Service of All the Dead

The King's Arms 26 Deadly Slumber *John Brewster leaves, followed by concerned girlfriend Jane Folley* 11 The Secret of Bay 5B *Morse chases Janice out into Broad Street*

Hertford Bridge 1 The Dead of Jericho 7 The Last Bus to Woodstock 31 Death is Now My Neighbour

New College Lane 4 The Wolvercote Tongue 17 Fat Chance 22 Happy Families 25 Absolute Conviction 31 Death is Now My Neighbour

The Turf Tavern 3 The Service of All the Dead *Morse leaves without drinking after seeing Ruth Rawlinson* 6 The Settling of the Sun

Mansfield Road 1 The Dead of Jericho

Holywell Music Room 28 Twilight of the Gods *Gladwys Probert gives a masterclass* 18 Who Killed Harry Field?

Wadham College 18 Who Killed Harry Field? 30 The Daughters of Cain 32 The Wench is Dead *Ian Matthews consulted about the paintings by Whistler and Durer*

University and Pitt Rivers Museums 30 The Daughters of Cain *A Rhodesian knife is stolen from a cabinet in the Pitt Rivers, Morse walks through the dinosaurs in the University Museum*

HIGH STREET WEST – CARFAX – CHRIST CHURCH – ST ALDATES AREA

The outstanding sites, Pembroke College (seldom open) and Tom Quad (entry charge), are not as accessible as most.

High Street 2 The Silent World of Nicholas Quinn 11 The Secret of Bay 5B *Pierce sells paintings* 17 Fat Chance 19 Greeks Bearing Gifts 24 Absolute Conviction 26 Deadly Slumber 31 Death is Now My Neighbour 33 The Remorseful Day *the anorak is left at a charity shop*

Covered Market 24 Absolute Conviction *the chase of Charlie Bennett ends with tea in Browns café* 19 Greeks Bearing Gifts *Maria gives Jocasta the slip*

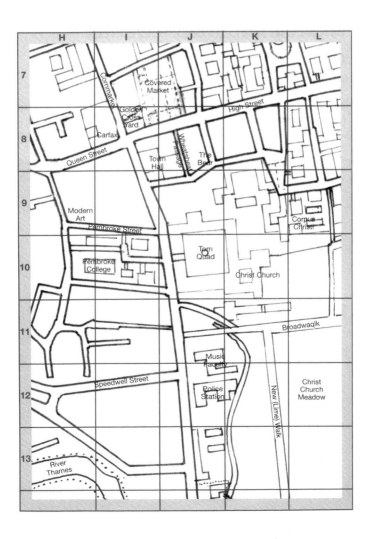

Opposite top: Oriel Square.
Opposite middle: Blenheim Park and the Grand Bridge.
Opposite below: Little Clarendon Street.

Right: Morse, Lewis and the Jaguar.
Below: Balliol College from Broad Street.

Carfax.

Wheatsheaf Passage – Gill & Co. 1 The Dead of Jericho *Lewis checks on Anne Staveley's keys* 7 The Last Bus to Woodstock *John Sanders smashes up tools display*

Carfax 9 The Last Enemy 19 Greeks Bearing Gifts 22 Happy Families 31 Death is Now My Neighbour

Town Hall Ballroom 11 The Secret of Bay 5B *Morse dances with Dr Russell*

Old Court Room 3 Service of All The Dead *trial of Ruth Rawlinson* 32 The Wench is Dead *trial of the boatmen*

Modern Art 18 Who Killed Harry Field?

Pembroke College 10 Deceived by Flight *Donn is murdered, The Clarets cricket team arrive* 18 Who Killed Harry Field *Lewis follows Tony Doyle towards gate house*

Christ Church Tom Quad 28 Twilight of the Gods *drinks party after the ceremony* 30 The Daughters of Cain *Morse is taken aback by Brownlee's attitude*

Christ Church Meadow 11 The Secret of Bay 5B *Morse and Lewis walk down New Walk* 28 Twilight of the Gods *Mari Probert walks with her boyfriend on Broad Walk*

88 St Aldates 26 Deadly Slumber *artist Wendy Hazlitt shows Morse one painting too many*

Police Station Various episodes, external view; also filmed in west London TA Centres.

JERICHO AREA

Between cosmopolitan Walton Street and the canal, with its painted narrow boats and wildfowl, are blocks of 19th-century terraces and many Morse sites from the early episodes.

Combe Road 1 The Dead of Jericho *Canal Reach, where Anne Staveley and George Jackson lived*

The Bookbinders Arms and Canal Street 1 The Dead of Jericho

The Jericho 2 The Silent World of Nicholas Quinn

Phoenix Cinema 2 The Silent World of Nicholas Quinn *where* The Last Tango in Paris *was shown, until Morse went to see it*

Le Petit Blanc 31 Death is Now My Neighbour *the ill-fated Geoffrey Owens entertains a girlfriend*

St Sepulcre's 32 The Wench is Dead *where Joanna Franks would have been buried, if dead*

Green College/Tower of the Winds 1 The Dead of Jericho 2 The Silent World of Nicholas Quinn

Radcliffe Infirmary 1 The Dead of Jericho 2 The Silent World of Nicholas Quinn 3 The Service of All The Dead 9 The Last Enemy 12 The Infernal Serpent 16 Second Time Around

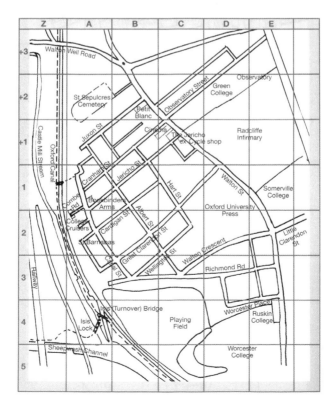

Top left: Trinity College as viewed from Broad Street.
Top right: Oxford Union Debating Chamber.
Above: Exeter College Front Quadrangle.

Opposite: Cloisters, Magdalen College.

MAGDALEN BRIDGE AREA

Magdalen College 1 The Dead of Jericho *Morse is attacked by Ned and later attends a talk by Tony Richards* 19 Greeks Bearing Gifts *Morse dines and meets Randall Rees* 28 Twilight of the Gods *Arabella's room is ransacked* 33 The Remorseful Day *Morse stands on a terrace overlooking the Cherwell*

Botanic Garden 2 The Silent World of Nicholas Quinn *Lewis catches up with Roope as he frames Bartlett* 6 The Settling of the Sun *Reverend Robson attacks a gardener* 10 Deceived by Flight *Donn eats fish and chips with Morse* 31 Death is Now My Neighbour

Magdalen Bridge 11 The Secret of Bay 5B *Henderson throws tape into the river* 4 The Wolvercote Tongue 6 The Settling of the Sun 31 Death is Now My Neighbour 33 The Remorseful Day 21 Dead on Time *Morse and Susan talk, later Lewis throws the tape incriminating Susan into the Cherwell*

Magdalen College School grounds/white bridges 31 Death is Now My Neighbour *Morse romances Adele Cecil*

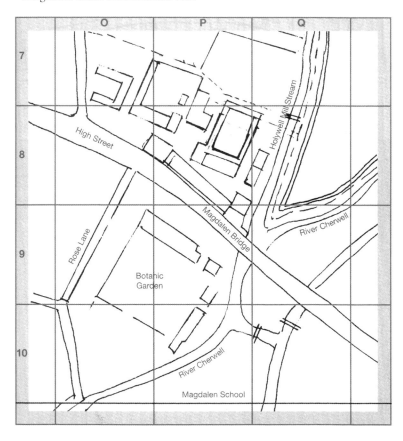

SHELDONIAN TO MERTON STREET AREA

It is difficult to single out one memorable Morse site from another in this area of spectacular architecture, but Radcliffe Square was the most used location in the series and if you have limited time, this is the area to cover.

Sheldonian Quad 1 The Dead of Jericho 8 The Ghost in the Machine 9 The Last Enemy *Morse and Lewis discuss the case and the Theatre's history* 21 Dead on Time 28 Twilight of the Gods *Gladwys Probert is shot*

Sheldonian Theatre 2 The Silent World of Nicholas Quinn 4 The Wolvercote Tongue 16 Second Time Around 21 Dead on Time *Morse takes old flame Susan to a concert* 28 Twilight of the Gods *witnesses to the shooting are interviewed*

Hertford College 7 The Last Bus to Woodstock 8 The Ghost in the Machine 21 Dead on Time

Left: Morse and Lewis.
(Courtesy ITV plc)
Below: St Aldates and Christ
Church.
Bottom: Fellows' Garden,
Exeter College.

Opposite: Magdalen College
Bell Tower from the water
walks.

Old Schools Quadrangle 6 The Settling of the Sun *Morse walks across, reading a programme* 24 Absolute Conviction *prison governor Mrs Stevens emerges and meets Morse* 28 Twilight of the Gods 32 The Wench is Dead

Radcliffe Square/Camera 1 The Dead of Jericho 6 The Settling of the Sun *the coach party arrives* 7 The Last Bus to Woodstock 8 The Ghost in the Machine 24 Absolute Conviction 28 Twilight of the Gods *Baydon arrives and leaves in a hurry* 29 The Way through the Woods 30 The Daughters of Cain *Ted Brooks' bloodstained bicycle is found* 31 Death is Now My Neighbour

Brasenose College 2 The Silent World of Nicholas Quinn *Morse attends dinner. Lewis starts his trail of Roope* 6 The Settling of the Sun *Morse gives talk to course students, interrupted by the murder of a Japanese student on the course* 9 The Last Enemy *John Gielgud, as the Chancellor, rehearses his speech about other Oxfords* 28 Twilight of the Gods 29 The Way Through the Woods 30 The Daughters of Cain 31 Death is Now My Neighbour

Brasenose Lane/ Exeter College wall 2 The Silent World of Nicholas Quinn *Roope stands below Lewis, who is above him on the wall*

St Mary the Virgin 2 The Silent World of Nicholas Quinn 6 The Settling of the Sun *All the aerial panoramic views*

The Bear (pub) 24 Absolute Conviction *Charlie Bennett goes through, pursued by Lewis*

Oriel College 2 The Silent World of Nicholas Quinn *discussion in the quadrangle* 8 The Ghost in the Machine *Dr Ullman gives a tutorial* 12 The Infernal Serpent *Dr Dear's funeral in the chapel, lunch afterwards in the hall* 26 Deadly Slumber *Morse walks through several quadrangles with Jane Folley* 28 Twilight of the Gods 31 Death is Now My Neighbour

Oriel Square 1 The Dead of Jericho 5 Last Seen Wearing *as she walks with Morse from Christ Church, Sheila Phillipson is identified by Lewis* 8 The Ghost in the Machine *Dr Ullman arrives at his college* 12 The Infernal Serpent 24 Absolute Conviction M*orse and Lewis seeing Bennett sitting on wall, start the chase* 26 Deadly Slumber 30 The Daughters of Cain

Christ Church gate and library 4 The Wolvercote Tongue 5 Last Seen Wearing *Morse and Sheila Phillipson emerge*

Merton Street 2 The Silent World of Nicholas Quinn *Morse is taken to the fictional Horse and Trumpet*

Corpus Christi 9 The Last Enemy *the main events, in the back garden and the cloisters*

Magpie Lane 26 Deadly Slumber

Merton College 3 The Service of All the Dead *Morse talks with the Archdeacon as they walk through the Front and Mob quadrangles* 12 The Infernal Serpent *the Master and Dr Dear leave in the rain from Patey's Quad; opening of parcels in the Fellows' Garden; Hopkirk smashes up flowerpots in the end scene*

WEST CITY AREA

Only keen location-finders will venture into this area, although the station was almost the most filmed of all the locations.

The Railway Station 2 The Silent World of Nicholas Quinn *Roope offers a lift to the Dean of Lonsdale College* 4 The Wolvercote Tongue *Howard Brown arrives from the Didcot Railway Centre* 8 The Ghost in the Machine *Lady Hanbury offers Betty Parker a lift, Morse also off the train* 16 Second Time Around 17 Fat Chance *Hilary Dobson's tampered bicycle is found* 18 Who Killed Harry Field? 30 The Daughters of Cain *Morse meets Kay Bach, takes her to The Victoria Arms* 32 The Wench is Dead *Morse sees Dr Van Buren off, meets Adele Cecil* 33 The Remorseful Day

Nuffield College 17 Fat Chance *Morse meets Emma Pickford in the Lower Garden*

Former Oxford Prison (now the Malmaison Hotel and 'Castle Unlocked' visitor centre) 29 The Way Through the Woods *Steven Parnell is stabbed to death after again denying the girl's murder* 32 The Wench is Dead *execution of the boatmen*

Westgate Car Park 11 The Secret of Bay 5B *Morse drives towards the entrance*

Oxford Union 12 The Infernal Serpent *Morse waits for Dr Dear to address the environmental debate* 19 Greeks Bearing Gifts *Randall Rees is insulted by students*

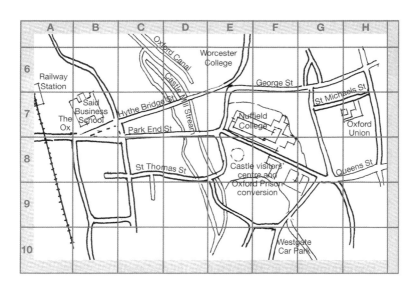

Left: Lewis and Hathaway. (Courtesy ITV plc)
Below: Pembroke College gatehouse.

Opposite above: Nuneham Courtenay Garden.
Opposite middle: St Giles' Fair carousel.
Opposite below: Broad Street.

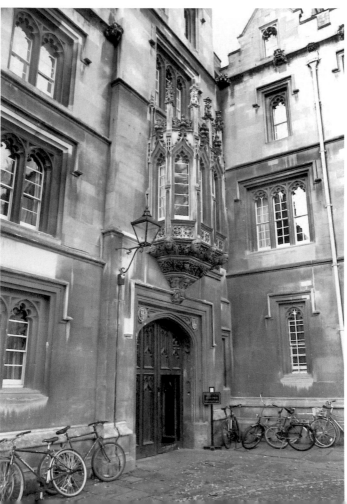

THE WATERWAYS

Oxford neglects its waterways, which flow around, but not through, the city. There are also very few places accessible to vehicles and most bridges are busy, so they are not ideal for body disposal. Nevertheless the filmmakers found them useful and distributed corpses evenly around the main courses, two in the Thames, two in the canal, and three, nominally, if not actually, in the Cherwell. There are continuous paths alongside the Thames & Oxford Canal. Some of the Thames side and millstreams are accessible.

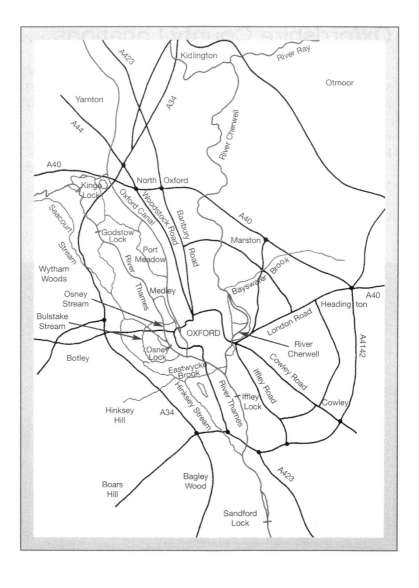

The Sandford Lasher (weir pool).

The River Thames 1 The Dead of Jericho *the Richards' house overlooks the river* 3 The Service of All the Dead *the Thames can be seen from the church tower (at Bray)* 4 The Wolvercote Tongue *the Tongue is recovered* 11 The Secret of Bay 5B *Manley is arrested in front of the boathouse* 26 Deadly Slumber *Aqualung equipment is found in Jane Folley's locker near Donnington Bridge* 30 The Daughters of Cain *Ted Brooks' body is found floating by a college boathouse* 33 The Remorseful Day *Harry Repps' body is found at Lower Wolvercote*

The River Cherwell 4 The Wolvercote Tongue *Theodore Kemp's body tumbles over the Weir* 11 The Secret of Bay 5B *Henderson throws an audio tape into the river* 10 Greeks Bearing Gifts 21 Dead on Time *Morse meets old flame Susan Fallon in Magdalen College water walks* 28 Twilight of the Gods *bodies are found* 30 The Daughters of Cain *Morse and Kay Bach are taken on a punt from The Victoria Arms* 31 Death is Now My Neighbour *Morse and Adele stand on the white bridge* 33 The Remorseful Day *another scene at The Victoria Arms as Morse and Lewis discuss the future*

The Oxford Canal 1 The Dead of Jericho *the canal reach cottages are by the canal* 9 The Last Enemy *Ballarat's body is found at Thrupp* 32 The Wench is Dead *scenes of the arranged 'murder'*

Opposite above: The High.
Opposite below: Folly Bridge and the head of
the river.

Top: Magdalen Bell Tower from the Botanic
Garden.
Above: Merton College from Christ Church
Meadow.
Right: Wadham College.

OXFORDSHIRE COUNTY LOCATIONS

Most of these are worth getting into a car to visit.

Blenheim Palace and Park and Woodstock (on A44 north-west of Oxford) 29 The Way Through the Woods

Burford (on A40 west of Oxford) 33 The Remorseful Day

Didcot Railway Centre (off A34 south of Oxford) 4 The Wolvercote Tongue

Nuffield Hospital, Headington 28 Twilight of the Gods   32 The Wench is Dead   33 The Remorseful Day

Lambourn and The Berkshire Downs (south-west of Oxford) 30 The Daughters of Cain

Nuneham Courtenay (south of the A423 Henley Road) 8 The Ghost in the Machine

Park Town (off Banbury Road) 29 The Way Through the Woods

Thrupp Canal Basin 9 The Last Enemy

The Trout and Godstow 4 The Wolvercote Tongue   16 Second Time Around 18 Who killed Harry Field? 33 The Remorseful Day

The Victoria Arms, Marston 18 Who Killed Harry Field?   30 The Daughters of Cain   33 The Remorseful Day

Wytham Woods and Village (referred to but not filmed) 11 The Secret of Bay 5B   29 The Way Through the Woods

PART 3

TOWN AND GOWN

This part gives a brief description of the Morse Oxford locations, as they were in early 2008. Contrary to its timeless image, both sides of Oxford are facing substantial pressures.

The town has to balance the interests of its citizens with those of the millions of visitors who come each year, and the 40,000 students at the two universities and other schools, resident for part of the year. After centuries of subjugation to the old university, most of the land, not only in the city centre, but outside it, is owned by colleges and the university. Unable to plan for a modern city, the town also failed to develop independent cultural and commercial facilities. Required to accommodate its tourists, it has to acknowledge that it is only the university that attracts them.

The university is at the heart of fierce political debate on the future of higher education. Historical accident has led to the spread over a wide area of hundreds of high-maintenance listed buildings and open spaces, and an expensive teaching style. If its student fees are increased to properly finance this privileged education, it may revert to the former elitism that it has tried to counter. If it is not allowed to charge viable fees, might it free itself of state funding, close itself off to the public, and stifle the tourism on which much of the commerce of the town depends?

THE TOWN

Pre-history: 200 million years ago the area was under the sea. There the coral formed into limestone, thrown up to form the Cotswold Hills, from which came the building stone for the great buildings of the university. The main drain from the hills, named the Thames, is believed to have flowed into the Rhine. When the land mass separated, it swung east to the North Sea, then about 10,000 years ago cut through the Chiltern Hills at the Goring Gap, and set its present course.

Pre-Middle Ages: the Romans distrusted the area, as it was cut by numerous streams and heavily wooded, and it was probably not until AD 700 that a significant Saxon settlement developed. It then lay between the kingdoms of Wessex and Mercia, and on the border with the eastern side of England under the Danes. The town layout had four roads crossing at Carfax, enclosed by a wall. The river would have spread shallowly across the wide flat valley, probably giving the settlement the name Oxenforde. Trading between Danish settlers and Saxons developed, but in 1002 the St Brice's Day Massacre saw the Danes imprisoned, then burnt in St Frideswide's Church. Retaliation followed, with Viking raids devastating the town and area for many years.

Norman period: after the Conquest Robert d'Oilli became Constable, the city wall was reconstructed and enlarged in stone, with a castle in the south-west corner incorporating the Saxon west gate, and a collegiate chapel for secular canons. To cross the Thames floodplain, a massive causeway, Grandpont, was built, on the line of the present Abingdon Road. Substantial abbeys grew up on the river and the monks and canons attracted students, forming the nucleus of the future university. In 1141, the civil war between Stephen and Matilda for the vacant crown reached Oxford. In 1142 Stephen laid siege, but Matilda escaped from the castle across the frozen river. There followed fourteeen years of civil war before Henry II, Matilda's son, re-imposed order.

The Normans recognised the area to be ideal hunting country, and several major lodges (palaces) were built, including Woodstock Manor and Beaumont Palace, where Richard 1 and probably his brother John were born. The surrounding countryside was forested and lawless.

Medieval period: the university developed slowly, hindered by the Black Death and other plagues, wars and town resistance. One group of scholars broke away to found, or join, Cambridge University. Perceived as part of the Roman Catholic Church, the university suffered at the 16th-century Reformation, but survived, except for the monastic colleges. The bishopric, previously at Lincoln, was transferred to Oxford in 1542, and in 1548 St Frideswide's Priory in Christ Church became the cathedral. The university was supported by Crown and Church in most disputes with the town, which gradually lost all the land east of the central road, and much of its civic authority. Only in the mid-20th century did the town begin to regain independence, although its current lack of facilities is a legacy of centuries of subjugation.

Pre-modern period: during the Civil War (1642-6) Oxford was the capital of the Royalists, who were supported by the university and, naturally, opposed by the town. Earthworks were thrown up outside the line of the Norman wall, a siege was laid, but Charles I fled without any serious fighting or destruction in the city. Cromwell became the Chancellor of the university during the Commonwealth and parliamentary sympathisers replaced many college Fellows and students. As at the Reformation, there was serious destruction by the Puritans of any item considered to be idolatrous. After the Restoration of Charles II, architects such as Wren, Hawksmoor and Gibbs began to design the great central buildings.

Social problems arose as people migrated from country to town. In 1790 the Oxford Canal reached the city bringing much-needed cheaper Midlands coal and other goods. Alongside it developed Oxford's first suburb, Jericho. Gas works came in 1819 and railways in 1844. In the late 19th century the Thames was engineered with a navigation channel and side streams.

Modern period: in 1912 William Morris, later Lord Nuffield, started production of Morris Cars in Longwall Street. When the car works, which at one time employed 35,000 workers, moved to Cowley, major suburbs developed around it.

Oxford Brookes University, previously the Oxford Polytechnic (1865-1970), has roughly 18,000 students on full- and part-time courses at Headington. It has a growing reputation in both vocational and academic subjects, attracts a substantial number of overseas students, and has a formidable sporting reputation. Adding to the student population, there are many other language schools trading on Oxford's reputation as the 'home' of the nation's greatest export, the English language.

The 'town' side of Oxford at last lives peaceably alongside the 'gown'. The car works is owned by BMW, there is much light- and science-based industry, and many people commute to London. The city centre has seen a massive development of flats, coffee shops, bars and fast food outlets, reflecting modern living. The world's cuisine can be sampled, not only in the centre but in ethnic Cowley Road and Jericho.

Right: Beautiful stained-glass window.
Below: Oxford statue.

TOWN LOCATIONS

Bear Inn (in grid K8 of the map on pages 8–9) the present site was part of a coaching inn on the High Street when, in 1606, it was an ostler's house, despite the sign proclaiming 1242. As a pub it was named 'The Jolly Trouper' in 1774 and 'The Bear' in 1801, from the emblem (a bear and ragged staff) of the 15th-century Earl of Warwick.

Beaumont Street to Wellington Square (G4–F2) Beaumont Street was built over the remains of medieval Beaumont Palace, where Richard I (Richard the Lionheart) and, possibly, his brother John were born. Palace remains can be seen from the rear alley, and cellars are still being found. The building was demolished in 1822 to make way for Beaumont Street. The Playhouse Theatre was where, in the book *The Riddle of the Third Mile*, St John's College student Morse met Wendy Spencer, who roomed by him in St John Street opposite. Their romance ruined both their degree chances. Behind is Burton-Taylor Theatre, for university drama training, financed by Richard Burton and Elizabeth Taylor after their appearance in *Dr Faustus* at The Playhouse.

St John Street was built in the 1830s of three-storey cellared terraced houses and leads to **Wellington Square**, built *c.*1870 and named after the Duke. Previously it had contained the 1772 workhouse for 200 paupers, and nearby was Rats and Mice Hill, a rodent-infested rubbish mound. In about 1970 the University Offices were set on the corner with Little Clarendon Street, and **Kellogg College** for continuing education is nearby.

Blackwell's Bookshop is one of the largest bookshops in the world and still a family firm. Starting in 1879 as a second-hand book dealer and lending library, it is now an international retail and publishing house. A Publishing division started in 1921, and an

Above: The Bear.
Right: Blackwell's Bookshop and the White Horse.

On-Line division in 1995. In Broad Street it has separate outlets for Music, Arts, Local History and Children's books, but its main store has a narrow, almost Dickensian front, giving no clue to the massive space behind it. This includes the 10,000 sq. ft underground Norrington Room, built in 1966, with 3 miles of shelving. On the first floor is a popular and very 'Oxford' coffee shop, in which, judging by the number of laptop computers on the tables, many dissertations are composed.

Blenheim Palace and Park and Woodstock 12th-century Woodstock Manor was built for Henry I in a royal hunting park. In it the Black Prince was born and Elizabeth I imprisoned. Partly destroyed when a Royalist outpost in the 17th-century Civil War, it was cleared when the Palace was built. A stone marks the site.

    Blenheim Palace, completed 1722, was a gift to the 1st Duke of Marlborough, John Churchill, and was designed by Vanbrugh and Hawksmoor, with a bridge across the River Glyme leading to the Column of Victory. In 1764 its formal gardens were converted to landscape style by 'Capability' Brown for the 4th Duke, forcing the sale of the Palace's lead roof to finance Brown's masterpiece. The valley was hand-excavated and clay-puddled, the bridge and part of the Manor's causeway, Elizabeth's Island, were retained, and the Glyme was dammed with a cascade. By The Lake is Rosamund's Well, romanticized as the bower of Henry II's mistress, Rosamund Clifford.

    Winston Churchill was born at the Palace in 1874, and is buried in nearby Bladon churchyard. The Italian and formal gardens by the Palace were formed in

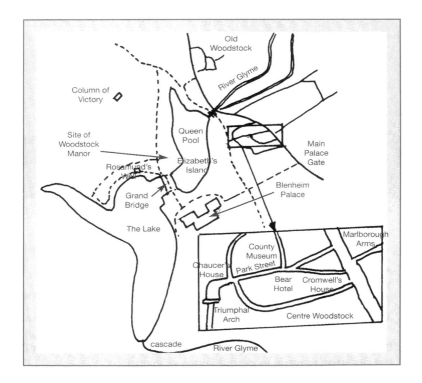

Blenheim/Woodstock.

the 1920s. Attractions such as a miniature railway and play areas have been added, and shows and events are held in the grounds.

Woodstock is mainly Georgian, with individual shops, restaurants and the county museum complete with stocks.

Open to public: dates and times vary **Entry:** £5 per car or £1 pedestrians **Tel:** 01993 811325 **www**.blenheimpalace.com

> **Also a location for:** *Young Winston* 1972, *Greystoke, The Legend of Tarzan* 1984, *The Avengers* 1988, *Black Beauty* 1994, *Hamlet* 1996, *The Four Feathers* 2002

Brasenose Lane (J–K6) links Turl Street to Radcliffe Square; it is the last city street to retain its central gutter, or kennel.

Broad Street (I–K7) In the Middle Ages ditches and possibly fish ponds lay outside the north city wall, but although the ground level would have been much lower than today, it would nevertheless have been too high for river water and so probably took local drainage and spring water.

The Martyrs' Cross marks the place where the Oxford Martyrs, Ridley and Latimer (1555) and Cranmer (1556), were burnt at the stake. Each year a wreath is placed by a motorcycling group in memory of a member who refused to wear a crash helmet. The model for the equally dead Harry Field in *Who Killed Harry Field?*

The Buttery was, at the time of filming, **Thornton's Bookshop** (est.1835), selling specialist books and catalogues.

The White Horse is an 18th-century timber-framed pub.

Tourist Information Centre from where guided Morse walking tours leave each Saturday at 1.30 p.m. **Tel:** 01865 250551

> **Also a location for:** Jude Fawley meets Sue Brideshead on the cross in *Jude the Obscure*, Thomas Hardy, 1896

Burford is a picturesque medieval wool town, known as 'The Gateway to the Cotswolds'. The main street runs down to a medieval bridge over the River Windrush. Nearby is a spectacular 'wool' church, a site of the suppression of the 'Levelers' mutiny' in the Parliamentary army.

Carfax (I8) was the central crossroads in Saxon times, the tower formerly part of St Martin's Church. On the south-west corner an inscription commemorates Swindlestock Tavern, where the St Scholastica's Day riot of 1355 started, the greatest of all the Town versus Gown conflicts, following which for 550 years the town was required to pay a penance to the university.

River Cherwell rises in Northamptonshire, and links for a short length to the canal. There was a failed attempt to make it navigable to Banbury in the early 18th century. Near Oxford it passes by The Victoria Arms, and enters the city spectacularly through the University Parks and the water walks of Magdalen College. The best Oxford punting is from Howards' boat station (tel 01865 202643) under Magdalen Bridge. Here the river is shallow and narrow, so it is never too far to wade to the bank, and there are always plenty of onlookers

River Cherwell
(Parson's
Pleasure),
University Parks.

to cheer or jeer! Beyond the bridge the river passes the Botanic Garden, and branches left past St Hilda's College. Near the Thames the river forks, the original course flowed right, directly against the flow of the Thames, which led to serious flooding. The new course to the left created Codgers Island, on which are the college boathouses.

Cornmarket (I6   8) was formerly North Gate Street; a corn market hall was erected in 1536 and demolished in 1644. Its lead roof was used to make Royalist bullets in the Civil War. The modern Cornmarket is architecturally undistinguished and often criticised. However, it is the only road with a view of the former position of the north and south gates of the old city wall, and contains one ancient pub and two outstanding buildings. The Crown, unobtrusively set down an alley, dates from 1032, becoming, in succession, Drapery Hall, Spicers Inn, The King's Head and, in 1600, The Crown. The buildings are the tower of St Michael at the north gate, Oxford's oldest structure dating from 1060 and at times part of the north gate of the wall, and the Bocardo Prison, both demolished in 1771. Opposite, on Ship Street, is a building with a projecting upper floor, possibly 14th century and once an inn. Stocks were removed from Cornmarket in 1810.

The surface of the street has often been the subject of controversy. In the Middle Ages cobbles sloped from the shop fronts to the centre gutter, and as the traders owned to the centre they often constructed cellars beneath the street, many of which were unearthed during resurfacing in 2003. Paving was laid in the 18th century and tramlines installed in the 19th. After the Second World War rubber blocks were laid in an attempt to absorb traffic vibration. In 1973 the street was partially pedestrianised. In 2001 expensive granite blocks began to crack, to public derision – BBC Radio 4 listeners voting it the second worst street in England!

Covered Market (J7) opened in 1774 to replace obstructive medieval street traders. Most of these were in Fish Street, now St Aldate's, Butcher Row, now Queen Street, and the Butter Bench in Carfax. In 1781 fruiterers moved in, but an attempt to house the corn market in 1850 failed for lack of space. The market, which against the trend closes on Sundays, was the primary supplier to the college kitchens. Wholesalers have encroached as the colleges have expanded, so now many shops supply the general public.

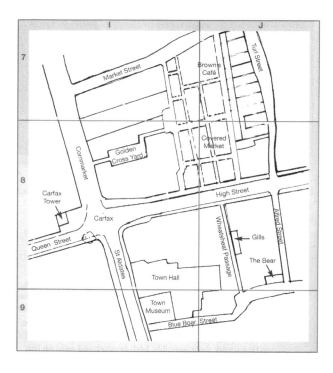

Carfax and
the Covered
Market.

Didcot Railway Centre is a magnet for railway enthusiasts, especially of steam. Admission charge is £6.50. There are various special days, including some that give the opportunity to drive a steam engine. The centre lies alongside Didcot Station.
  Tel 01235 817200 **www**.didcotrailwaycentre.org.uk

The Eagle and Child (G2) (aka 'The Bird and Baby') started in 1650, named after the family crest of the Earl of Derby. Perhaps because it is larger internally than the outside suggests, it has become the HQ of the Dr Who Appreciation Society, and naturally they call it 'The Tardis'. It is better known for the meetings in the Rabbit Bar of the Christian writers' group The Inklings, which included C.S. Lewis and J.R.R. Tolkien. Visitors to the pub between 1930 and 1960 might have taken little interest in a group of middle-aged men eating their traditional cheese sandwiches and reading to each other. They would have been surprised to learn that one would write, by popular vote, our favourite book, producing Oscar-garlanded films, another the Narnia books on which Disney Studios are to base a series of films in the first decade of the 21st century.

Golden Cross Yard (J8) is approached either from the Covered Market or off Cornmarket through a 15th-century gateway. It has been largely rebuilt since its 12th-century origin. Its restoration was inspired, like that of many other buildings, by John Ashdown, formerly the city conservation officer. Shakespeare is thought to have stayed in a 16th-century painted room, formerly of The Crown Tavern, now forming part of the Pizza Express restaurant. Shakespeare's godson William Davenant, nominally son of The Crown's landlord in the 17th century, later became

Above: Wheatsheaf Passage.
Left: Golden Cross Yard.

a playwright and poet laureate, and claimed to be Shakespeare's illegitimate son. The yards of coaching inns such as this were often used for the performance of plays and shows, so it is likely that Shakespeare and his 'Kings Men' troupe entertained here.

High Street (aka The High) (I–P8) The curving line of this famous road is believed to follow the old cattle drovers' track as it took the gradient out of the slope from the Cherwell valley up to Carfax. At one time it was called Eastgate Street. Magdalen, Queen's, University, All Souls', Lincoln and Brasenose colleges and St Edmund's Hall all flank it. Notable buildings include Magdalen bell tower, The Queens with its baroque façade, the Examination Schools, and St Mary's and All Saints' Church (now Lincoln's library). Entry to St Mary's is through the eccentric and catholic baroque porch of 1630 that incensed the Puritans and influenced the impeachment and execution of Archbishop Laud. No. 106–7 is still identifiable as a medieval academic hall, Tackley's Inn. The Grand Café is on the site of the first coffee house in England, then the Angel Inn (1651). Medieval shops, often very narrow, lined the west end within the wall. In 2000 the Oxford Transport Strategy closed the road to public daytime traffic with the construction of a visually ruinous central bus gate.

Off the High Street is **Wheatsheaf Passage.** Gill & Co., founded 1530, claim to be the oldest ironmongers in the UK. The Passage also has The Wheatsheaf pub with a jazz club, and a French bistro.

Jericho and environs (E2) Jericho was Oxford's first suburb. It is probably named after an inn, *Jericho*, which offered rooms to travellers from the north and west who were too late to get through the city gates before they closed. *Jericho*, taken from the parable of The Good Samaritan, was a name often given to such an inn near a walled town. The present pub dates from 1818. It replaced a building dating from 1650, which was probably on the site of a medieval inn. The pub has had various names, including simply *Jericho*, also *Jericho House, Jericho Tavern*, and in the mid-1990s *The Philanderer and Firkin*. Now it has reverted to *The Jericho*.

Although Jericho was largely uninhabited until the early 19th century, there were several important 18th-century adjoining developments, including Radcliffe Infirmary and Worcester College 1714.

In 1790 the **Oxford Canal** arrived in Oxford, to link to the national canal system the River Thames and the River Trent. It brought vital trade and boatmen and canal workmen, 'navvies' (navigators), some of whom settled in the area. Jericho turned into a mini-port, with a red-light district on Walton Street. The most notable industry to develop alongside the canal in 1825 was **Lucy's Eagle Ironworks**, now mainly closed, followed in 1826 by Clarendon Press, later **Oxford University Press**. Terraced artisans' houses were developed on a grid pattern. The canal cut off natural drainage to the Castle Mill stream, resulting in flooding, pollution and major cholera epidemics, and many left the resulting slums. Thomas Combe, superintendent of the Press, and a supporter of the high-Anglican Oxford Movement, became a benefactor, providing schools and **St Barnabas Church** 1869.

The modern Jericho, with its chequerboard Flemish bond terraces, has become fashionable, a mix of workers, students, artists and professionals. The main street to the east, Walton Street, now has a number of smart restaurants in addition to the cinema, pubs and cafes. Jericho benefited from the concern caused by the clearance of another suburb, St Ebbes, and became a conservation area that received international acclaim. Down Richmond Road a Lebanese restaurant lies opposite a synagogue, embodying the spirit of cosmopolitan Jericho.

Old Bookbinders Ale House (formerly The Bookbinders' Arms), is one of only six pubs in Jericho. At its peak there were 24. Some were for specific trades, like The Bookbinders', which opened shortly after the University Press moved to Jericho (1826–51). The internal scenes in *The Dead of Jericho* were not filmed here.

Combe Road, opposite The Bookbinders', is a short cul-de-sac that originally led to a chain ferry across the canal. It was named Ferry Road until 1959. College Cruisers boatyard is now at the end. It was renamed Canal Reach in the film.

The **Phoenix Cinema** started in 1913 as the North Oxford Kinema, for silent films with a 3-piece orchestra. It became The Scala in 1920, and then in 1970 Studio 1 & 2 with a cinema club called Studio X. In 1977 it took its present name and is now Oxford's 'art cinema' with two screens.

Le Petit Blanc, Walton Street, a fashionable bistro founded by celebrity chef Raymond Blanc.

St Sepulcre's was one of three cemeteries opened in the 1850s (the others at Holywell and Osney) to relieve overfull churchyards. The immediate need was to bury victims of cholera epidemics, but pressures on burial space had increased, as pre-Reformation shrouds were replaced by graves with headstones. The cemetery stands on the site of the then abandoned Walton Manor Farm and is accessed through a Gothic-revival gateway of 1865. Surprisingly large, and not attached to a church or chapel, it attracts attention from property developers.

Little Clarendon Street, now a trendy shopping street, has always been an important link between the area of the present Jericho and the city. In the Civil War it was Black Boy Lane, named after the swarthy Charles II, and then in 1771 Workhouse Lane, leading to the workhouse in Wellington Square. In 1850 it became Little Clarendon Street and was rebuilt in the 1970s, with Somerville College on the north side.

> **Also a location for:** Jude Fawley lived in Jericho in *Jude The Obscure*, Thomas Hardy, 1896, *Lyra's Oxford*, Philip Pullman, 2003

The King's Arms (K4) 1607 was named in honour of James I. In the 17th century plays were performed here, by 1771 it was a coaching inn on the London to Gloucester run. The premises are owned by Wadham College and its students have rooms on the upper floors. It is a very popular student pub and coffee house.

Lambourn and The Berkshire Downs This is a major centre for horse racing with a number of important stables.

Magdalen Bridge (Q9) lies alongside a ford, perhaps the original 'Ox ford'. The first bridge, in 1004, was timber and called East and Pettypont. In the 16th century it was replaced by a 150m-long stone construction. Before river improvements, flooding often reached to the bridge top, necessitating frequent repairs. Rebuilding was financed by tolls supplemented by Magdalen College and the university; widening took place in the 19th century. Zenith Films, makers of the *Morse* series for Central TV, financed parapet renovation in the 1990s. Boats, including the traditional but awkward punts, can be hired (01865 202643).

   Also a location for: *Iris* 2001

Magdalen College School (Q9) started as a grammar school within Magdalen College, but became independent by the 17th century. After the Second World War it became a direct-grant school, in 1976 an Independent. It has over 600 boy day pupils, and choristers sing on the college tower on May morning. Playing fields are accessed by the white bridges between branches of the River Cherwell.

Magpie Lane (L8) links High and Merton Streets. It has been called Grope (dark and disreputable) Lane, then Grape Lane, Winkin Lane and then, in the 17th century, Magpie Lane, after an alehouse. It later became Grove Street before 'Magpie' was readopted. It is bounded by Oriel College and University College, ex-President W.J. Clinton roomed in Kybald Street in 1968.

Mansfield Road and Lower Holywell Street (M1–4) This apparently unexceptional area almost uniquely links old and new Oxford. Within the 14th-century New College is the best remaining part of the 12th-century city wall. Holywell Street has mainly Georgian houses, including The Alternative Tuck

The King's Arms.

Shop and a Japanese homemade food restaurant. J.R.R. Tolkien lived at No. 99 between 1950 and 1953. On the left up Mansfield Road, laid out in its present form in 1887, are the Gothic-revival buildings of 19th-century Harris Manchester and Mansfield Colleges, founded for non-Conformists. Opposite is the 1989 School of Geography. Across the south of Mansfield College some traces still remain of the earthworks thrown up by Royalist defenders in the 17th-century Civil War. On the right is Balliol College's sports ground. The road terminates in the modern era as it passes the Institute of Virology and enters the science area.

> **Also a location for:** Balliol's ground was the site of Shrewsbury College in *Gaudy Night*, Dorothy L. Sayers, 1935

Martyrs' Memorial (H5) was erected in 1841 on the site of the Robin Hood Inn, in high Gothic style to the design of an Eleanor Cross, and commemorates the protestant Martyrs executed in Broad Street. Construction was funded by public subscription, to counter the high church 1933 Oxford Movement. So much money was raised that the Church of St Mary Magdalen was extended with the surplus. Limestone lasts barely 150 years in exposed conditions and predictably in the 1990s the structure was crumbling. As no money had been set aside for maintenance, and as no one had a strong claim to ownership, it took some years to effect a restoration, but in 2002 it was finally completed. Colin Dexter presided at the unveiling.

Merton Street (formerly St John Baptist's Street, Jones Street, Coach and Horses Lane) Mainly cobbled, flanked by ancient buildings, this is a favoured site for historical film makers. From Oriel Square two colleges, Corpus Christi and Merton, are on the right, divided by a path that leads down through the south city wall. Merton's 13th-century chapel has a line of distinctive gargoyles, now redundant. Opposite is the side of Oriel College chapel and two late 13th-century halls, Beam and Postmasters, which housed Merton's undergraduates until 1575. Set into the back of University College is Merton's Real Tennis Court, where the archaic game can be watched, if not understood. Further on is the Philosophy School and an exit from the Examination Schools, where final-exam students are exuberantly greeted by their friends, hence glitter in the cobbles! Round the corner is No. 21, where J.R.R. Tolkein lived and wrote, the Eastgate Hotel, marking the line of the old wall, and opposite the ornamental side of the Examination Schools.

> **Also a location for** *Oscar and Lucinda* 1996, *The New World* 2006

The Mitre High Street (J7) The hostelry dates from 1310 and was named after the mitre of the Bishop of Lincoln. Lincoln College is the current owner. It became a centre of Roman Catholic resistance to the Anglican Reformation through the 16th and 17th centuries, and was often attacked for this reason. It sits over cellars even older than the inn, probably medieval tradesmen's stores, and used for secret masses. Stories of escape tunnels radiating from the inn are traditional but unproven. It was a bustling coaching inn in the 17th century before the advent of the railways. It is currently a Beefeater Inn.

New College Lane (L5) wriggles down from Catte Street to The High, changing to Queen's Lane halfway. It is barred to through traffic, so is a pleasant and interesting short walk as long as bicycles are avoided. Of note are Hertford Bridge, Halley's House, the Industrial Revolution black-grimed walls, the summer entrance to New College, the row of grotesques on the college, the Provost's lodgings and classical library of The Queen's College, St Edmund's Hall and the ever-popular coffee house on The High.

> **Also a location for:** Disguised as a Chinese road in *Spy Game* 2002; Harriet Vane accepts Lord Peter Wimsey's proposal here in *Gaudy Night*, Dorothy L. Sayers, 1935, *Love in a Cold Climate* Nancy Mitford, 1949, *Zuleika Dobson* Max Beerbohm, 1911

Nuneham Courtenay (off A423 Henley-on-Thames road) The first Earl Harcourt built the house from 1714 with a classical English garden by Capability Brown. In the grounds are the disused All Saints Church, in the style of a Greco-Roman temple, the Temple of Flora, and various urns. In a nearby field, overlooking the Thames, stands the remains of the Carfax Conduit 1610 which once brought water to the city from Hinksey Hill. In 1760 the old village was demolished and rebuilt on the main road, where there is also an arboretum owned by the university, the present owner of the house. The current tenant is the Global Retreat Centre, who may give permission to visit (01865 343551).

Oriel Square (L8) is distinguished, or some say vulgarised, by Oriel's taste for pastel colours on the north side buildings, which are linked by a tunnel to the main college. A traffic gate set across the square in 2002 has not enhanced its appearance.

Oxford Canal (E6 – A1) This is one of the Midland narrow canals, about 5m wide and 1.5m deep. It draws its water from reservoirs to the north, and some land drainage, and connects to the Cherwell to the north and the Thames twice, once through Duke's Cut, Wolvercote, built for the Duke of Marborough, and finally via the Sheepwash Channel near the railway station. It arrived in Oxford in 1790 and brought vital supplies of coal and industrial products, but its viability was threatened by the Grand Union Canal, which avoided the costly Thames locks on the way to London, and then by the railway. As the economics declined, boatmen were forced to live and work on their boats, and so they ornamented what had become their homes by painting on them roses, castles and other traditional patterns. Much of this artwork was over-painted in British Waterways' colours at nationalisation. The canal basin was filled in and developed by Nuffield College.

The modern canal has more boat movements than in its industrial heyday, but virtually all are recreational and houseboats, with some boats servicing the houseboats, and the craft of British Waterways. There is a continuous towpath, offering land-based recreation for walkers, cyclists and anglers – and of assistance to murderers wishing to dispose of bodies!

Oxford Castle and Prison (F8) This area has been the site of an invader's castle, a court, prison cells long before HM Prison (1888–1996), executions, plagues, official and unofficial burials, and even a famous curse. No wonder this had the

Oriel Square from the north end.

Oxford Prison, St George's Tower and Castle Mound.

Park Town crescent.

reputation as a dark and terrible place, and it required imagination, some say insensitivity, to turn it into the pleasure ground it has now become. The castle mound, tower and some former cells are a visitor attraction, Castle Unlocked, offering a depressing account of man's inhumanity. The 4-star Malmaison Hotel (2005) converted some cells into luxury rooms, albeit with the original cell doors and barred windows, and there is a range of restaurants around it.

The castle was constructed by the Normans shortly after the Conquest, and would have started as a quickly constructed motte (mound) with keep on top, and a fortified bailey around it for men and livestock. The tower would probably have existed marking the west gate in the Saxon wall. As the stone city wall was gradually built, the site was incorporated into it, and a moat linked to the 11th-century Castle Mill Stream. Mottes were formed of layers of earth and stone, for drainage into the moat, so interfering with the drainage causes instability, as can be seen. The keep is no longer there, but the well shaft is. The site had a prison from 1166 and held rebellious students from 1236.

During development, sixty macabre skeletons from the 16th and 18th centuries were excavated from the filled moat, some almost certainly remains from dissections by the university anatomists. The early ones are thought to be from those who died from a curse laid on the court, the Black Assizes, in 1577 by a convicted heretic. Mystery surrounds this, but somehow the remains were unceremoniously dumped there. For more information, google 'the curse of Oxford gaol'.

For more information visit the web site of the Oxford Archaeological Group, www.oxfordarch.co.uk.

> **Also a location for:** *A Fish Called Wanda* 1988, *102 Dalmations* 2000, *Wilde* 1997, *Spy Game* 2002, TV several episodes of *The Bill*. *Ancestors: The Curse of Oxford Gaol* 2004, Book: *An Instance of the Fingerpost* by Iain Pears.

Park Town off the Banbury Road 1853, partly crescents of 3-storey houses.

The Railway Station (A6) Around 1840 two factions tried to prevent the railway coming to Oxford. One was The Oxford Canal Company, which correctly saw its nemesis looming. The other was the university, which feared for the morals of its students, the effect on drainage, and social problems if the 'lower orders' could move about. Nevertheless in 1844 the GWR line reached Oxford, the station at Western Road, then followed in 1851 by LNWR; its station on the Rewley Abbey site with a design similar to Crystal Palace. In 1852 GWR moved to the present station site. LMS took over LNWR in 1922, and after the 1948 nationalisation the LMS station and line were closed, and the swing bridge over the Sheepwash Channel made a national monument. The station was rebuilt in 1971 and in 2000 the old distressed LMS station was removed to a museum (despite some protest) after which Saïd Business School and new roads were constructed.

The station was almost the most used Morse location, mostly showing miscreants pretending to alight from a train to establish a false alibi, as if Morse would be deceived!

Randolph Hotel (H5) was built in Gothic revival style in 1866 and extended on a number of occasions. This prestigious hotel is now part of the Macdonald group and has 109 bedrooms. Most of the cast and crew of the *Morse* series stayed here, as did people temporarily evacuated if their houses were used for locations. The former Chapters Bar has been renamed The Morse Bar, and cocktails available include *Morse's Special, Dexter's Choice* and *Chief Superintendent Strange*. The foyer has been redesigned since it was first shown in *The Wolvercote Tongue*. In The Morse Bar and dining room there is a superb collection of photos from the series, and Colin Dexter pops in regularly.

Tel: 0870 400 8200 **www**.macdonald-hotels.co.uk

> **Also a location for:** C.S. Lewis meets Joy Gresham in the lounge (the actual meeting was in The Eastgate Hotel) *Shadowlands*, 1994

St Aldate's (J8 – 14) is believed to be the city's first street, leading from Wessex across the south Thames crossing, now Folly Bridge, formerly Grandpont. Here was possibly the ford for cattle, the Ox-ford. It is not known who Aldate was, or if he or she existed. From 1300–42 the street was called Great Jewry, after the Jewish quarter inside the south gate, then Fish Street after the fish market. It now has the law court, police station, Alice's shop, Pembroke College, St Aldate's Church and the gates of Christ Church.

In the Middle Ages this road and its extensions north divided the university on the east side and the town on the west side, with the poorest quarter west of St Aldate's. Trill Mill Stream was a major branch of the River Thames outside the wall, until pollution by butchers and tanners who lined its banks polluted it to the point where it had to be culverted.

St Giles (H2 – 4) is the widest street in Oxford. St Giles' Church at its north end has been restored often since its foundation in 1133. In the Civil War parliamentary prisoners were held there, and it was damaged in the siege. St Giles' Fair is held in the first week of September. It started in 1634 as a parish feast, became a children's fair in the 1780s, developed for adults with sideshows such as freaks and bare-knuckle boxing, but now offers mainly high-tech stomach-churners for adolescents, and a cherishable carousel. Opening on to St Giles are St John's College, St Cross College, the Modern Languages Faculty (Taylorian) and The Eagle and Child.

St Mary Magdalen (I5) is an important historic building. A church has stood on the site since 1074, and the present church has been variously extended from the 16th centruy. Its extension, using spare money from construction of the Martyrs' Memorial, made it wider than it is long. Graveyards at both ends were only begun in the early 19th centruy, on the site of houses, an academic hall, shops and Robin Hood Inn. The church's position, at the entry to the north gate of the city wall, was important to travellers and traders.

Ship Street (I – J6) was a medieval lane, variously named, that once wound across the city, through Catte Street and on to the East Gate, past the sheep market and the Sheep Alehouse. It was probably orignally named Sheep Lane, then Ship Lane and finally, by 1850, Ship Street. Now shortened by Exeter College at its east end, and bounded by Jesus College on its south side, it starts with Oxford's oldest standing building, the tower of St Michael (c. 1050) at the North Gate.

Shirburn Castle is a fortified moated manor house near Tetsworth, Oxon, dating from 1378. Formerly privately owned by the Earl of Macclesfield, it contained one of Britain's most important privately owned libraries, auctioned in 2004 after a family feud that might have inspired *Happy Families*.

   Also a location for: *Portrait of a Lady* 1996

Summertown closely followed Jericho as a suburb in 1820. It has varied architecture and a lively shopping centre.

The River Thames (rows 13 – 14) The source lies some 35 miles to the west, with spring-fed streams converging to form the main river, navigable up to Lechlade. By the time it has reached central Oxford it has passed through 12 locks and fallen 17m in level reaches. The river was crucially important in the development of the town and the university, providing a route to London and attracting abbeys and teaching friars. For centuries it was poorly administered, with frequent disputes between millers and bargemen, and it frequently dried up or flooded. Finally in 1790 a navigation channel was agreed, and pound locks began to replace the dangerous flash locks, the first in 1632. The river is now administered by the National Environment Agency, although the side streams are owned and theoretically maintained by the riparian owners.

When it arrives on the wide flood plain the river breaks up into a number of side streams, most of them man-made mill cuts from the 11th century, and all with weirs falling to match the nearest lock. Weir gates are operated by the keepers at each lock, with telemetry linking to the HQ at Reading.

The main river slips by the old city of Oxford up on its hill, but regularly floods those properties that have risked building on its floodplain. College rowing regattas take place between Iffley Lock and Folly Bridge, the boats rowing one behind the other and trying to 'bump' the boat ahead. There are two links to the canal, the main one through the Sheepwash Channel. All the old bathing places have been closed for safety reasons, but the water is purer than for centuries and fish ladders are being set into the weirs to allow salmon to return to the headwaters. The Thames Path runs almost continuously to London.

The River Thames through Oxford is sometimes called The Isis, a romantic but unofficial name coined in the 18th century.

Also a location for: *Three Men in a Boat* Jerome K. Jerome, 1889

Thrupp Canal Basin (north of Kidlington) A short lane off the A423 runs past The Boatman pub and alongside the Oxford Canal and over a bridge to a British Waterways depot. Well below the canal level is the River Cherwell, which, a short distance north, joins the canal. Across the water meadow is the deserted plague village of Hampton Gay. A short distance further north occurred one of the greatest railway disasters at Shipton-on-Cherwell when, on Christmas Eve 1874, a train derailed, causing 35 deaths.

Town Hall (H8) The site was in the medieval Jewish quarter, and has had civic uses since the 13th century. The present hall dates from 1897, built over a 14th-century crypt now containing the city plate, above which are various panelled rooms including a hall used for meetings and dances, and the former courtroom, closed 1969. In 2004 there is debate over the future use of the building. The excellent **Town Museum** is in the south-west corner.

Open to public: Tuesday to Friday 10–4.30, Saturday 10–5, Sunday Noon–4 **Entry:** £2 **Tel:** 01865 252761

Also a location for: *A Fish Called Wanda* 1988, *Kavanagh QC* 19??

The Trout Inn, and Godstow This historic and beautiful area can be reached from Oxford by road or by a rewarding walk on the Thames Path.

The lock In 1894 the Thames Conservancy was authorised to replace the flashlocks and install pound locks on the upper Thames. Godstow Lock, falling 1.6m, and the navigation channel bypasses, were constructed in 1928.

Godstow Nunnery The lock channel cut through the burial ground of the Benedictine Nunnery, founded in 1133, disturbing a number of lead coffins. Nothing remains of the original buildings. The present ruins are post-15th century. The Nunnery would possibly have been small and unimportant but for the chance meeting in 1150 of the 17-year-old future Henry II, hunting from Woodstock, and the 15-year-old Rosamund Clifford, who became his mistress. When Henry for political reasons married Eleanor of Aquitaine four years later, Rosamund returned to the Abbey and Henry made it wealthy, a fact that, after Rosamund's death, did not impress the Bishop of Lincoln, who threw out her venerated remains. Two hundred years later a monk, who created the legend of 'The Fair Rosamund', romanticised the story. Her ghost is said regularly to walk the river path. The Abbey was dissolved at the Reformation and later further ruined in the Civil War. Charles 1 would have seen it as he fled from Oxford across nearby Port Meadow in 1646. English Heritage currently manages the ruins.

Godstow Bridge The older section is 15th century, and would have seen much skirmishing in the Wars of the Roses and later in the Civil War. On her first entry into Oxford, university representatives met Elizabeth I on the bridge. They possibly had some misgivings after the burning of the Protestant Martyrs in the reign of her sister Mary.

The Trout Inn This uniquely beautiful inn sits above a secondary lock by-pass. From the long riverside terrace can be seen the medieval bridge, the weir with a fall of 1.6m, and a restored timber bridge crossing to an island. Peacocks parade on the terrace, and shoals, mainly of chub, swim below the bridge. There may have been a hospice for visitors to the Nunnery on the site, but the present building was a fisherman's house in the 16th century,

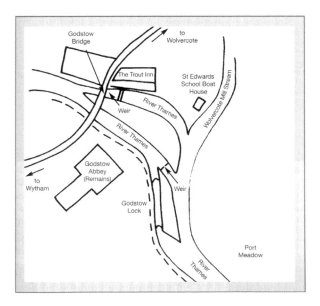

The Trout/
Godstow Priory.

until it became an inn in 1625. It was largely rebuilt in 1737 and extensively modernised in 2001.

At the far end from the entrance is an area with interesting Morse memorabilia. Before reaching it there is the original photograph of Colin Dexter used on his book covers, and a blackboard with an extract from J.R.R. Tolkien, who is buried in nearby Wolvercote Cemetery. Below, there are more original Morse photographs, and a wall cabinet containing an imaginatively assembled collection of memorabilia. This includes the original Jaguar handbook; Morse's warrant card, signed 'Morse'; bottles of real ales; a Rachmaninov piano concerto tape; a crossword and documents from the early series. The inn also owns the buckle made for *The Wolvercote Tongue*, recovered in the film by a frogman near the bridge.

The Trout is part of the Mitchell & Butlers group, one of their Vintage Inns.
Open: 11–11 Monday to Saturday, noon–10.30 Sunday **Tel:** 01865 302071

> **Also a location for:** *The Saint* 1999, *The Inspector Lynley Mysteries* 2004. It was on boat trips to Godstow in 1862 that Lewis Carroll entertained Alice Liddell and her sisters with stories that became the famous *Alice* books.

Turf Tavern (L6) (between Holywell Street and New College Lane) was first a malt house, then a cider house in 1775, before becoming the Spotted Cow Inn in 1790, and finally the Turf Tavern in 1790. It lies under the north wall of the city and is a favourite student pub. Accessed by narrow passages, it is so celebrated it appears to need no signs to indicate its presence. On the wall of an outer area is a blackboard recalling the pub's *Morse* connections.

Turl Street (J5 – K8) is an ancient street between High and Broad Streets, probably named after a former twirling gate in the north city wall. There are individual shops and the gates of Lincoln, Jesus and Exeter colleges.

The Victoria Arms (aka The Vicky) The isolated position, reached through Old Marston village, is due to an old ford, and a former line-ferry across the

The remains of Godstow Nunnery.

Cherwell that closed in 1971. The present building dates from the 17th century and was closed between 1958 and 1986. It is unlikely that a punt with boatman could be hired here, as Morse did with the delectable Kay Brooks in *The Daughters of Cain*.

Westgate Multi-storey car park (G10) The 'Bay 5B' sign is absent. Maybe taken by a Morse fan, maybe never there. This unlovely building is due for redevelopment, but meanwhile there are panoramic views from the roof.

Woodstock Road (G1) The only way in and out of Oxford, without crossing a river and flood plain, is north, but in that direction there were no major cities comparable to London, Winchester and Gloucester, nor navigable waterways until the Oxford Canal. Most of the present road was not developed until the 19th century, when large houses were built for college Fellows and businessmen, some of which have been acquired by the university or converted into flats. Then followed women's and graduate colleges, St Edward's School, a radiator factory and other development.

Broughton Castle near Banbury, is a spectacular moated manor house dating from AD 1300, crenellated in 1406 but never a military castle. In 1377 it was owned by William of Wykeham (New College), related to later owner Sir William Fiennes, Lord Saye and Sele, and it is still owned by the Fiennes family. It was a centre for parliamentary resistance to Charles I, and after the Battle of Edgehill (1642), was captured by the Royalists. From this period there are connections with the start of Yale University at Saybrook, Connecticut.

Actors Ralph and Joseph and explorer Ranulph are among a number of high-achieving Fiennes.

Occasionally open to the public, it has a small restaurant. **Tel/Fax:** 01295 276070 **www**.broughtoncastle.demon.co.uk

> **Also a location for:** *Shakespeare in Love* 1998, *Joseph Andrews* 1977, *Lady Jane* 1985, *Three Men and a Little Lady* 1990

The Victoria Arms.

THE GOWN

Formative period: the university is believed to have originated in AD 1100 when students began to gather in Oxford, some living in abbeys and monastic institutions, others staying in Academic Halls under a Master, or even more informally. The university was chartered in 1213. The first colleges were founded from the mid-13th century, mainly by high churchmen, often bishops, and took older scholars, sometimes founders' relatives, from their dioceses. In 1139 the Church enforced celibacy on priests, so colleges up to the Reformation were often bequeathed money and land. Young students were confined to the Halls, until New College became the first to admit them in 1379. Gradually the better-endowed colleges absorbed the Halls and other land to establish the present boundaries, and most have substantially reconstructed their buildings as student numbers have increased. The history of many of them is complicated, and there is no apparent consistency in the, now official, dates of their foundation, as they emerged from Halls to Colleges, evolved or became re-founded.

Middle period: the university, mostly taking only Anglicans from an elite sector of society, declined between the 17th and 19th centuries, and has been described in that period as a combination of clerical seminary and upper-class finishing school. Decline of college income was hastened by 19th-century agricultural depression. As the university became decadent, so nostalgia for it grew. Poets and writers, such as Lewis Carroll and Matthew Arnold, created the idea of a golden city, although this had little to do with the town. Late 19th-century reforms, forced through by the government, have brought in new types of students, non-Anglicans from 1871, women with their own colleges in the 1880s, scientists, overseas students and, increasingly, state school pupils. Many of the tutors were clerics waiting to be offered a parish living, but when Fellows were allowed to marry, tuition became professional. Between the two world wars the university entered its 'Brideshead' phase, dominated in the public eye by upper-class young men, who took partying more seriously than studying.

Modern period: colleges, except for some of those only for graduates, are multi-disciplined. All but one of the colleges are co-educational and, except for some graduate colleges, they are not specialist in a subject. Some have extra-curricula reputations, for arts or sport, although these distinctions are fading. After the Second World War new types of college were founded, designed non-traditionally, mainly for postgraduates in the burgeoning sciences. Competition for places has become more intense; students are now admitted on academic ability only, and on an assessment of their suitability to benefit from the Oxford style of tuition. There are now 39 colleges joined in a federation to form the University of Oxford. They are registered charities, governed by tutors elected to be Fellows, who in turn elect a head. From these usually, but not always, comes the Vice-Chancellor, and there is a titular head, the Chancellor, elected by the Master of Arts.

The university: administers the curriculum and subject faculties, examines and awards degrees, runs the museums, central and faculty libraries. It is increasingly an internationally important research centre, and assists the formation of commercial enterprises to exploit its research. The Oxford University Press is a successful and lucrative combination of academia and business.

Admissions and teaching: undergraduates usually apply to a college, which must have a tutor in their subject. Their choice may be influenced by family, school or friends, by prospectuses and visits, or by the character of the college. Undergraduates, if accepted, are admitted first to the college, and then matriculated to the university. Postgraduates are first admitted to the university, and then allocated a college. Teaching in the college is currently by small group tutorial, for about one hour per week per subject, and attendance is compulsory. Lectures take place in the faculties administered by the university, and attendance is optional. Students in the traditional Arts subjects are more college-based, Science and Medical students more involved with the faculties and teaching hospitals. The university is continuously adapting to outside influences, remodelling its curriculum, admitting a greater variety of students on short courses, and mature students through its Department of Continuing Education. It offers many scholarships and bursaries, including the world-famous Rhodes scholarship. See Part 4 for a statistical summary.

Buildings and gardens: most of the central buildings are built of limestone. The earliest that survive are designed in medieval Gothic, which was continued in 'revival' style into the modern era. Restoration architects, such as Wren and Hawksmoor, favoured classical designs. The old colleges were based on narrow buildings without corridors, forming open squares, known as quadrangles. W.H. Butterfield parodied all these in his 1870 Keble College, combining brick, Gothic revival, corridors and quadrangles. Keble later added notable modern buildings, as did other colleges and the university faculties. Lawns now common in the Front Quads are mostly recent additions, since the areas ceased to be working spaces. The gardens were, until the 17th century, used for food and medicinal herb production, and in medieval times occasionally for burial. Most have now adopted the English informal style.

Extra-curricula activities: colleges compete with each other at sport. Rowing is prominent, the races held on the river, single file, the boats trying to 'bump' (overlap) the one in front. The results can be seen chalked on college walls, if they have had success. The best sportsmen compete against Cambridge University, for which they receive a 'Blue' or 'Half-Blue' or 'Colours'. There are no sports scholarships. There are over 200 societies offering a wide range of activities, including the Oxford Union for politics, and many choral, drama and national groups. Students are generous in their support for the local hostelries, despite every college having its own bar.

Oxford and Morse: approximately one third of the various criminals in the *Morse* series were portrayed as heads or Fellows (dons) of these ancient institutions; their real-life counterparts tolerated with equanimity and humour the predominately unflattering portrayal of them. The remaining rogues from the town and country were usually middle and upper class. There was nothing

Morse liked more than 'fingering the collar' of his social superiors! Although not always supplying the criminals, colleges were featured in all but six of the thirty-three films.

The closed and intellectual college communities have always attracted storytellers, especially crime writers. Most have portrayed the students as effete and upper class, and the Fellows as unworldly but respectable. Although such stereotypes do occur in the *Morse* series, we also see working-class students and dons guilty of every form of base criminality, pursued by a cultured introspective policeman, one as unlikely as the other. Only the famous buildings that ornament most episodes remain aloof. Did the college authorities realise how they would be caricatured when they took the location fees, and will they ever take such risks again?

COLLEGES

Colleges are open to visitors at their discretion and, unless stated, by prior arrangement. Most colleges, appreciative of the public money that supports them, are generous in allowing access. Where times and costs of access are given, they are for guidance only. Student numbers were approximate in 2004, postgraduates include Additional Students.

The first section below details the seventeen colleges that were Morse locations, none were called by their real names. Following this are brief details of the other twenty-two colleges, some of which appeared in background scenes.

BALLIOL COLLEGE

FOUNDED	1263 BY JOHN DE BALLIOL
OPEN TO PUBLIC	OCCASIONALLY
ENTRY	CHARGES APPLY
TEL 01865 277777	WWW.BALLIOL.OX.AC.UK

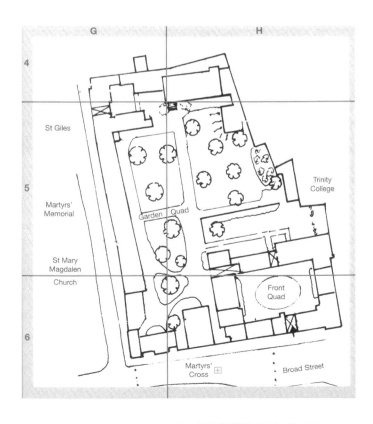

The college first occupied humble buildings outside the city wall. At the Reformation it remained staunchly Roman Catholic. Its Master was appointed Bishop of Gloucester under Mary I. He was involved in condemning the Oxford Martyrs, who were burnt outside the old college gate in 1555–6; the scorched door hangs in the north-west corner of the Front Quad. Fire intervened again when in 1666 the Great Fire of London burnt down the college's London property, the subsequent loss of rents impoverishing it. Recovering, it led 19th-century academic reforms and gained a reputation for high-scholarship, which it still retains. In the 1960s it had a radical left-wing bias, was among the first to admit women, and is now involved and active in university affairs. It is said that 'Balliol men achieve effortlessly', and now, presumably, women do too.

Balliol has a traditional and generally good-humoured rivalry with its neighbour Trinity, for example once attempting to 'sell' Trinity, although between 1877 and 1941 they shared a science laboratory.

ALUMNI SELECTION
Matthew Arnold, John Evelyn, Gerald Manley-Hopkins, Hillaire Belloc, Julian and Aldous Huxley, H.P. Hartley, Graham Green, Anthony Powell, Neville Shute, Herbert Asquith, Lord Beveridge, Harold Macmillan, Vincent Massey, Sir Edward Heath, Sir Seretse Khama, Sir Denis Healey, Chris Patten, Roy Jenkins, John Wyclif, Adam Smith, Benjamin Jowett, Arnold Toynbee, HM The King of Norway, Princess Hawada of Japan, George Carman, Richard Dawkins, Kevin and Ian Maxwell.

ALSO A LOCATION FOR
The college of Lord Peter Wimsey in *Gaudy Night*, Dorothy L. Sayers, 1972.

BRASENOSE COLLEGE (AKA 'BNC')

FOUNDED	1509 BY WILLIAM SMYTH, BISHOP LINCOLN AND SIR RICHARD SUTTON, LAWYER
OPEN TO PUBLIC	10 – 11.30 (GROUPS) 2 – 4.30/5
ENTRY	VARIABLE GROUP CHARGES
TEL 01865 277830 WWW.BNC.OX.AC.UK	

The founders were two men from Lancashire and Cheshire. They converted a 13th-century academic hall, Brasenose, to a college, and absorbed several others. The hall's name came from a leonine-ringed doorknocker, and one enduring story is that when the students fled the riots in Oxford in 1333 to set up a university in Stamford, Lincolnshire, they took the knocker with them, but left it behind when later forced to return to Oxford. In 1890 the college bought the house to which the knocker was attached, and bringing it back to Oxford hung it over the high table in the dining hall. There is doubt whether this is the original knocker.

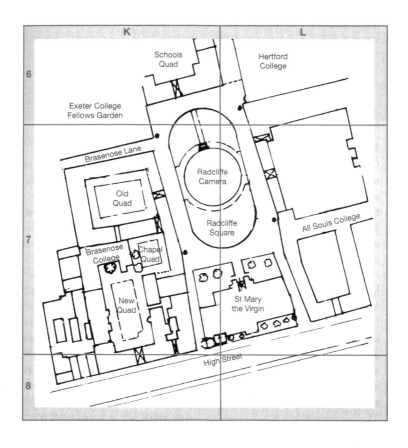

The college survived the Reformation and the Civil War, and by the early 17th century had a Puritan reputation, to be followed by Jacobite leanings at the end of that century. In the 19th century it was favoured by the 'squirearchy', obstructed university reform and became known for its sporting excellence. It is now middle of the road, low politically and sport-wise. Although work is taken seriously, the students' prospectus says that 'a healthy proportion of students find it easy to ignore BNC's proximity to the Bodleian Library'. The college boasts a famous snack bar called Gerties.

One 16th-century Principal, Alexander Nowell, accidentally invented bottled beer but surprisingly has been given no memorial.

ALUMNI SELECTION
John Buchan, Robert Burton, John Foxe, Michael Palin, William Golding, John Mortimer, Jeffrey Archer, Sir Arthur Evans, William Webb-Ellis, Colin Cowdrey, Earl Haig, Robert Runcie, Richard Bellingham, Richard Mather, Lawrence Washington.

ALSO A LOCATION FOR
Tom & Viv 1994 (*also see* Merton).

CHRIST CHURCH (AKA 'THE HOUSE') AND MEADOWS

FOUNDED	1525 BY THOMAS WOLSEY AS CARDINAL COLLEGE, IN 1532 IT BECAME HENRY VIII's COLLEGE AND CHRIST CHURCH IN 1546
OPEN TO PUBLIC	MOST DAYS 9–5.30, SUN 12–5.30 HALL OFTEN CLOSED 12–2
ENTRY	CHARGES APPLY

TEL 01865 276492 WWW.VISITCHRISTCHURCH.NET

PICTURE GALLERY, ORIEL SQUARE TEL 01865 276172

WWW.CHCH.OX.AC.UK/GALLERY

Founded on the site of an Augustinian Friary, the priory became Oxford Cathedral in 1542, the bishopric transferring from Lincoln, and uniquely the Dean, head of the college, administers the cathedral. The site is historic. In 727 St Frideswide founded her convent. In 1002 the St Brice's Day Massacre occurred (see 'About Oxford'). The main Jewish quarter was in the area from early 12th century to their expulsion in 1290. During the Civil War 1642–6 the college was the court of the King and Royalist Parliament met in the hall.

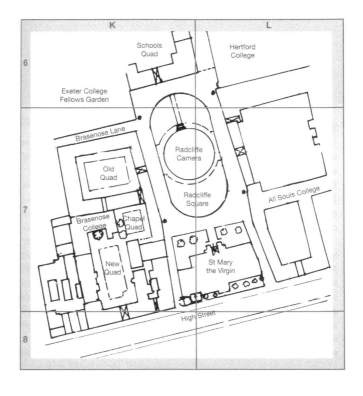

Having connections with Eton College, Christ Church has always been aristocratic and powerful, producing fourteen British Prime Ministers. More than any other college, it is geared to tourism, relying on it to finance maintenance of its historic buildings, and has a film theatre and shop. Its Picture Gallery, for which a separate entry charge is made, can also be accessed from Oriel Square. The college's two main popular attractions are its 'Alice in Wonderland' memorabilia and recently its association with the *Harry Potter* films. It has a preparatory choir school and an internationally known choir.

Christ Church Meadow is on the flood plain of the Thames, and, until 19th-century river engineering, was covered by side-streams and marshes. The Cherwell forms the eastern boundary; the causeway of Broad Walk separates the Meadow from the playing field of Christ Church School and the south city wall. New Walk, down which Lewis Carroll, Alice Liddell and her sisters walked on the momentous 1862 river trips, is the western causeway, beyond which is Trill Mill Stream. The Meadow is the summer home of the college's herd of long-horned cattle.

Most of the college boathouses are at the bottom of Christ Church Meadow on Codgers Island, which is formed by the old and new branches of the Cherwell. The boathouses downstream at Donnington Bridge are mainly for the town and Oxford Brookes University.

Providing a pleasant walk, a path leads from the Botanic Garden alongside the Cherwell and Thames, and then either up New Walk or through to Head of the River pub.

ALUMNI SELECTION
PMs Gladstone, Peel, Elgin, Canning, Halifax, Salisbury, Eden, Penn, Shaftesbury and Douglas-Home, John Locke, Phillip Sydney, John Pusey, John and Charles Wesley, Edward VII, The Crown Prince of Jordan, Charles Dodgson (aka Lewis Carroll), W.H. Auden, Henry Acland, Nigel Lawson.

ALSO A LOCATION FOR
A Yank at Oxford 1938, Alice's visit to New York in *Dreamchild* 1985, *Brideshead Revisited* TV series 1982, *Oxford Blues* 1984, *Harry Potter and the Philosopher's Stone* 2001, *Harry Potter and Chamber of Secrets* 2002, *The Dinosaur Hunters* 2002, *The Golden Compass* 2007, *Alice in Wonderland* Lewis Carroll 1865, *Jude the Obscure* Thomas Hardy 1896, *Brideshead Revisited* Evelyn Waugh 1945.

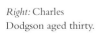
Right: Charles Dodgson aged thirty.

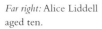
Far right: Alice Liddell aged ten.

CORPUS CHRISTI COLLEGE

FOUNDED   1517 RICHARD FOXE, BISHOP OF WINCHESTER
OPEN TO PUBLIC   1.30 – 4.30
TEL 01865 276700 WWW.CCC.OX.AC.UK

Bishop Foxe intended to found a monastic college but fortunately, in view of the impending Reformation, was persuaded to make it secular. Influential statutes compared college life to being a bee in a hive. It was the first college to be set up under the influence of the Renaissance, and possessed an important library of humanist texts. However, although Foxe was a widely travelled Renaissance man, his primary concern was with orthodox religion. During the Civil War, the college uniquely retained its silver, and the courts of the King (in Christ Church) and of the Queen (in Merton College) passed through the back garden.

The college remains small, friendly and, some say, insular, with a high proportion of overseas students and a keen attitude to both sports and the arts. The Front Quad remains paved and therefore has a more sociable atmosphere than those with lawns on which only the Fellows can tread. It is dominated by the Turnbull Sundial (1581), on the top of which is the bishop's symbol, the pelican. The pretty back garden is a mix of cultivated and wild plants and the path at the top of the south city wall gives a great view across the meadows and to the back of the cathedral, especially after dark.

ALUMNI SELECTION
John Keble, Matthew Arnold, Robert Bridges, Isaiah Berlin, William Waldegrave, John Ruskin, Lord Beloff, C.P. Scott, James Oglethorpe (founder Georgia USA).

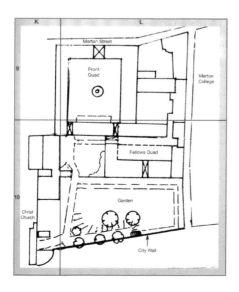

EXETER COLLEGE

FOUNDED   1314 WALTER DE STAPLEDON, THEN REFOUNDED BY
WILLIAM PETRE 1566

OPEN TO PUBLIC   2 – 5

TEL 01865 279600 WWW.EXETER.OX.AC.UK

The college started as Stapledon Hall, for poor boys from Devon and Cornwall. It became Exeter Hall in 1405 and, after languishing through the Middle Ages, Exeter College in 1566. Most buildings are from that period or later, excluding the old gatehouse, Palmers Tower (1432). The beautiful Gothic-revival chapel is the third on the site, and dominates the Front Quad. The Fellows' Garden gives a panoramic view over Radcliffe Square. The students are appreciative of the fact that the college's central position makes it within stumbling distance of Oxford's finest clubs and pubs. It has a musical and artistic reputation, reflected by its excellent graffiti proclaiming success in college rowing.

ALUMNI SELECTION
Tariq Ali, Martin Amis, Roger Bannister, Alan Bennett, R.D. Blackmore, Tina Brown, Edward Burne-Jones, Richard Burton, Lord Fisher, Russell Harty, Liaquat Ali Khan, William Morris, Hubert Parry, Philip Pullman, Ned Sherrin, Imogen Stubbs, J.R.R. Tolkien

ALSO A LOCATION FOR
'Jordan College' in *The Northern Lights*, Phillip Pullman, 1995, made into the film *The Golden Compass* 2007.

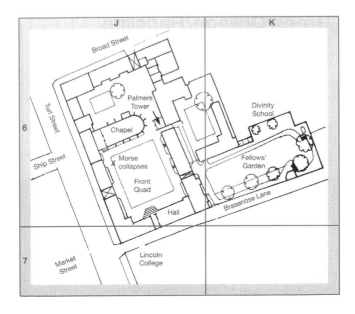

GREEN COLLEGE/RADCLIFFE
OBSERVATORY (WOODSTOCK ROAD)

FOUNDED   1977 BY DR CECIL AND MRS IDA GREEN
OPEN TO PUBLIC   BY ARRANGEMENT
TEL 01865 274770

Dr Green, the founder of Texas Instruments, was inspired by photos of the landmark Observatory to finance a graduate college for medical students that would incorporate the building. The university dislikes over-specialised colleges, and as a wide range of studies has been admitted, the medics have formed Osler House within the college to separate them from other students.

James Wyatt completed the Radcliffe Observatory in 1794. On top is 'The Tower of the Winds', based on an Athenian horologium. Atlas and Hercules support the globe. Architecturally splendid, it was never an exceptional observatory and ceased to be as such in 1935, when it became used for university medical research, which moved to the James Radcliffe Hospital (JR2). There are plans to merge with Templeton College.

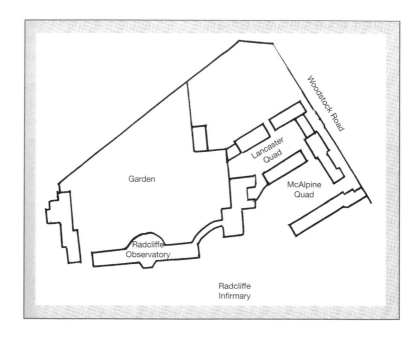

HERTFORD COLLEGE

FOUNDED   1740 BY RICHARD NEWTON
OPEN TO PUBLIC   10 – 12 2 – DUSK, MAX GROUP 10
TEL 01865 279400 WWW.HERTFORD.OX.AC.UK

This has the most convoluted history of any college and has appropriately ended up with the quirkiest set of buildings, most of which, including the landmark Bridge of Sighs (1913), were designed by Sir T.B. Jackson in the Palladian style known as Anglo-Jackson. The chapel is severe (as is the inside of the bridge), and contains a remarkable Tyndale window, set against a wall. Even the date of the college foundation is debatable; it could equally be 1283, the official 1740, or 1874. Some attributed alumni actually went to Hart or Magdalen Halls, from which the college sprang. When it was Hart Hall, it was a refuge for crypto-Catholics, but when it was refounded with finance from T.C. Baring, it defied the Test Act for Religious Tolerance by restricting entry to Anglicans.

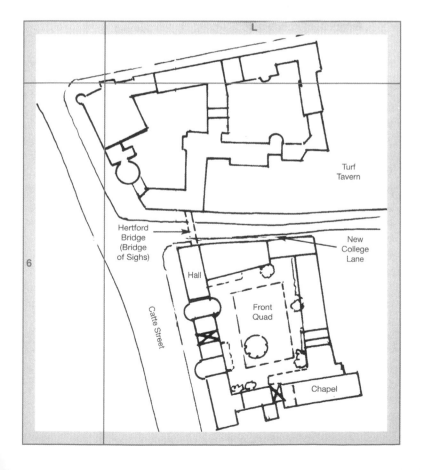

As though influenced by its history and buildings, the college has a reputation for freethinking and innovation. It was in one of the first groups to admit women and to establish the now-defunct entrance examination. It takes an unusually high proportion of state school, northern and female students. It is known to be friendly, slightly left-wing and unpretentious, and every successive college cat is called Simpkins.

ALUMNI SELECTION
John Donne, Charles Fox, Jonathon Swift, William Tyndale, Evelyn Waugh.

ALSO A LOCATION FOR
The college of poor student Charles Ryder in *Brideshead Revisited* Evelyn Waugh 1945.

MAGDALEN COLLEGE

FOUNDED   1458 WILLIAM OF WAYNFLETE, PROVOST OF ETON
OPEN TO PUBLIC   OCT 1–JUNE 24 1–6 OR DUSK; JUN 25–SEP 30 12–6
ENTRY   CHARGES APPLY
TEL 01865 276000 WWW.MAGD.OX.AC.UK

The college was founded to educate men for the State, rather than the Church. It suffered loss at the Reformation and the Commonwealth. Built outside the city wall on a key position on the east route, it absorbed the 13th-century St John's Hospital, some buildings of which remain. The bell tower was used as a lookout in the siege of the Civil War and is a landmark at the eastern approach to the city. There is a preparatory school 1480 and internationally famous choir, and a deer park from 1705. The New Building (1733) standing alongside the deer park was

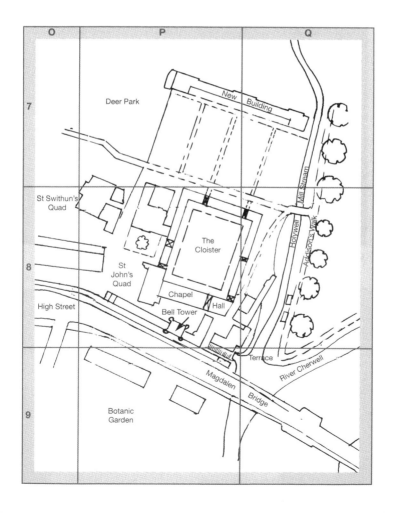

planned to be the start of a massive quad to rival Tom Quad of Christ Church, covering the area of the cloisters. The planned development fortunately did not happen, so the building stands isolated, its wings still awaiting the extension. On May morning, choristers sing from the top of the bell tower as the sun rises, while an attentive audience crowds the High Street, the most foolhardy or inebriated of which climb drainpipes and jump into the river.

The water walks by the branches of the Cherwell are spectacular in the spring. Gatecrashers, desperate to get into the celebrated Commemoration Ball, have been known to try to wade across the Holywell Mill Stream. Magdalen has a tradition of working and playing hard, within a lively supportive community.

Note: Magdalen is pronounced 'Maugdlin' and Cherwell is pronounced 'Charwell' – essential knowledge if you don't want to sound like a tourist!

ALUMNI SELECTION
John Betjeman, Crown Prince of Japan Chichubu, Howard Florey, Edward Gibbon, William Hague, John Hampden, Ian Hislop, Sir Keith Joseph, C.S. Lewis, Compton McKenzie, Dudley Moore, Desmond Morris, Ivor Novello, A.J.P. Taylor, William Tyndale, Oscar Wilde, Thomas Wolsey.

ALSO A LOCATION FOR
Accident 1967, *Shadowlands* 1994, *Howards End* 1991, *Wilde* 1997, *White Mischief* 1987, *A Fish Called Wanda* 1988, *Hercule Poirot*, *Jack the Ripper* 1988, (Professor Anthony Smith was Director of the British Film Institute 1979-88).

MERTON COLLEGE

FOUNDED	1264 BY WALTER DE MERTON, BISHOP OF ROCHESTER
OPEN TO PUBLIC	WEEKDAYS 2 – 4, WEEKENDS 10 – 4
	OLD LIBRARY TOURS ON OCCASION
TEL 01865 276310 WWW.MERTON.OX.AC.UK	

Merton contests with University and Balliol for the title of oldest college, and is so in terms of its model statutes. Founded for secular clergy, to curb the power of the Oxford religious orders, it later had a high scientific reputation. Always comparatively wealthy, the college has been able to preserve and maintain its buildings to a high standard. Mob Quad, dating from 1307, is the oldest Oxbridge quadrangle. The beautiful library, the oldest in the UK, is in the south-west corner. The chapel has notable stained glass, and once had a separate street door for the parish. The outstanding Fellows' Garden is closed to the public, except for open days and plays.

Merton is small enough to be friendly, large enough to have space. It is academically pressing, but uses its wealth to provide excellent facilities and care for its students.

ALUMNI SELECTION
Sir Basil Blackwell, Max Beerbohm, Sir Thomas Bodley, Randolph Churchill, T.S. Eliot, William Harvey, Jeremy Isaacs, Kris Kristoffersen, Robert Morley, Crown Prince Naruhito, J.R.R. Tolkien, Anthony Wood.

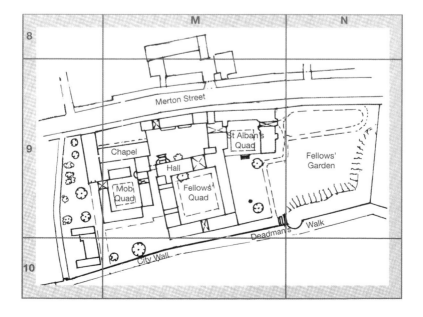

Merton College from Christ Church Meadow.

ALSO A LOCATION FOR

Oscar and Lucinda 1996, T.S. Eliot's marriage in *Tom & Viv* 1994, *Black Beauty* 1994.

NEW COLLEGE

FOUNDED   1379 WILLIAM OF WYKEHAM, BISHOP OF WINCHESTER
OPEN TO PUBLIC CHARGES APPLY
ENTRY   REMAINDER 2 – 4 HOLYWELL STREET
TEL 01865 279555 WWW.NEW.OX.AC.UK

The Bishop was the son of a Hampshire peasant, and rose to become Lord High Chancellor and surveyor to the royal castles. He acquired a site in the north-east corner of the city depopulated by the Black Death, and set up the college to provide educated men for Church and State, taking students from his other foundation, Winchester College. The revolutionary quad layout became a model for other colleges, with a great chapel back-to-back with the oldest Oxbridge dining hall. The chapel contains Epstein's 'Lazarus'; El Greco's 'The Apostle James', the founder's crosier, and beautifully carved seats with misericords along the back rows. Within the cloisters was held the Royalist arsenal in the Civil War. Until 1834 the college awarded its own degrees. The best-preserved section of the 12th-century city wall encloses the garden. Like Christ Church and Magdalen, there is a preparatory school and a famous choir. The college had strong 20th-century left-wing connections, welcomes state school pupils, and has a celebrated bar.

ALUMNI SELECTION
Kate Beckinsale, Tony Benn, Isaiah Berlin, David Cecil, Richard Crossman, Angus Deayton, John Fowles, Hugh Gaitskell, John Galsworthy, Hugh Grant, A.P. Herbert, Julian Huxley, Douglas Jay, Lord Longford, Len Murray, Dennis Potter, Sydney Smith, Mel Smith, Reverend W.S. Spooner, Rick Stein, George Woodcock.

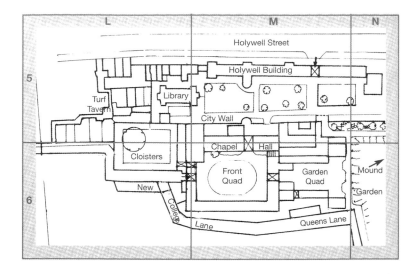

New College Garden Quadrangle.

Chapel windows.

ALSO A LOCATION FOR

James Bond has a Danish lesson here, advancing the cause of the individual tutorial before being interrupted in *Tomorrow Never Dies* 1997, Michael Palin's grandfather Reverend Frank Ashby has a choice to make in *American Friends* 1993, the story of De Sade in *Quills* 2000, *Cold Lazarus* 1996 (Denis Potter), murder, and a 16th-century dinner in the dining hall in *An Instance of the Fingerpost* Iain Pears.

NUFFIELD COLLEGE

FOUNDED   1937/1958 WILLIAM MORRIS, VISCOUNT NUFFIELD
OPEN TO PUBLIC   BY ARRANGEMENT
TEL 01865 278500 WWW.NUFF.OX.AC.UK

Lord Nuffield used his fortune made from his Morris Motors car works to fund many Town and Gown institutions and this is his college, although it was a university department until 1958. He originally wanted it to be for engineering and accountancy but was persuaded that it should be for Social Studies. Early relations between Lord Nuffield and the college were often strained. At one point he is quoted as describing it as 'that bloody Kremlin where left-wingers study at my expense', but later he added substantially to his bequest.

Building began in 1949 on the site of the disused Oxford Canal Basin. Its main feature is the tower, which contains the library and was the first to be built for 200 years. The large pool in the Lower Quad reflects the origin on the canal basin. The small upstairs chapel contains exceptional stained-glass windows by John Piper and Patrick Reyntiens.

The college was by far the first to admit both men and women, and was the first graduate college since All Souls. One aim was to create a college for non-academic visiting Fellows, to bridge the gap between the outside world and academe. Another was to improve the city approach from the west, but that

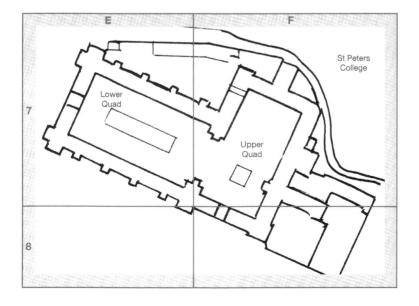

Lower Quad.

is probably beyond redemption. The college owns most of the area around it, including the Worcester Street car park, which produces an annual income of £1.3m and is valued at £23m. Cost will probably mean that plans to restore the canal basin will never be realised.

ALUMNI SELECTION
John Birt, Nigel Lawson, David Butler, David Howell, A.H. Halsey

ORIEL COLLEGE

FOUNDED   1324/6 BY ADAM DE BROME, REPLACED BY EDWARD II

TEL 01865 276555   WWW.ORIEL.OX.AC.UK

The 14th century was disastrous for plague, famine and war, and also for Edward II, who claimed to be the college founder in 1326, a year before he perished painfully in Berkeley Castle. It absorbed three academic halls, and appointed the vicar of St Mary the Virgin. Unlike most early colleges, it was not notably regional. The medieval buildings were replaced in the 17th century, and produced a spectacular Front Quad with the statues of Edward II and Charles I (or possibly James I) over the entrance to the hall.

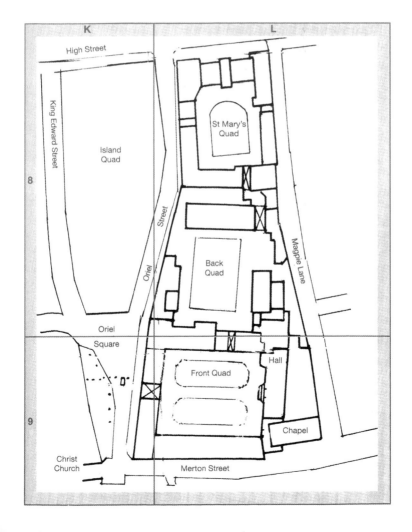

The college was reluctant to accept the Reformation and tunnels, probably originally made to aid the escape of priests, run from it to nearby sites. It was the home of the high-church 19th-century Oxford Movement, and the last to admit women in 1984. It is the top men's rowing college, dominating inter-collegiate rowing in recent times.

ALUMNI SELECTION
Thomas Arnold, Matthew Arnold, Beau Brummel, Lord Fairfax, Thomas Hughes, Sir Thomas More, Sir Walter Raleigh, Cecil John Rhodes, Gilbert White.

ALSO A LOCATION FOR
Hugh Grant's first film *Privileged* 1982, *Oxford Blues* 1984, *True Blue* 1991, *The Dinosaur Hunters* 2001.

PEMBROKE COLLEGE

FOUNDED	1624 THOMAS TEESDALE, RICHARD WIGHTWICKE AND WM HERBERT, 3RD EARL OF PEMBROKE
OPEN TO PUBLIC	BY ARRANGEMENT
TEL 01865 276444 WWW.PMB.OX.AC.UK	

Built on the site of twelve medieval halls, poorly endowed, the college was at the vanguard of the 19th-century reformist movement, and refused to accept low-quality students. It has a strong rowing tradition and a reputation for informality and friendliness, owing much to its strong international contingent, particularly American. The McGowin family of Alabama donated the library and has sent nine sons to the college. Pembroke continues to be poorly endowed, but always puts on a charming floral display in its compact Front Quad in summer, which also has a memorial plaque to James Smithson.

ALUMNI SELECTION

Senator J.W. Fulbright, Michael Heseltine, Samuel Johnson, John Pym, James Smithson, Oz Clarke.

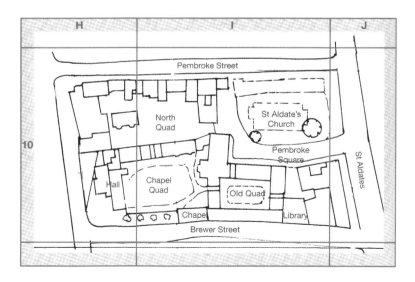

TRINITY COLLEGE

FOUNDED   1554 SIR THOMAS POPE, LAWYER
OPEN TO PUBLIC   10 – 12 2 –4 WEEKENDS, TERM 2 – 4
ENTRY   £1.50 WITH CONCESSIONS
TEL 01865 279900 WWW.TRINITY.OX.AC.UK

The college selected students from the landed gentry and certain schools, to educate them for secular state service. On the site of former Benedictine Durham College 1286, Sir Thomas Pope acquired his fortune administering the seizure of Roman Catholic property. The Civil War siege ended with one Trinity man surrendering to another. The Grove had a reputation during the war for dueling and romancing. The Garden Quad is mainly the design of Sir Christopher Wren. The chapel of 1691 was the first classical design, very daring for a religious building, and contains magnificent woodcarving, possibly by Grinling Gibbons.

ALUMNI SELECTION
John Aubrey, Sir Richard Burton, Anthony Crosland, Lord Goddard, Miles Kingston, J.H. Newman, Lord North, William Pitt the Elder, Terence Rattigan, Jeremy Thorpe.

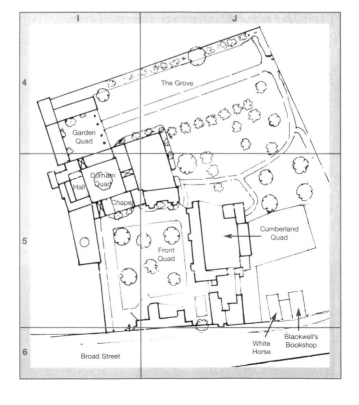

UNIVERSITY COLLEGE (AKA 'UNIV')

FOUNDED   1249 WILLIAM OF DURHAM
OPEN TO PUBLIC   SELDOM, BY ARRANGEMENT
TEL 01865 276602 WWW.UNIV.OX.AC.UK

The college moved to its present site in 1380, absorbing four halls. In 1361 a land dispute led to it forging documents, which stated that its founder was Alfred the Great. In 1872 it celebrated its millennium! The mainly 17th-century buildings include a chapel with magnificent Abraham Van Ling windows (1641). The domed roof of the memorial to Percy Byshe Shelley (1894) can be seen from the High Street, and earlier here were the laboratories of Robert Hooke and Robert Boyle (1665–8). It was a military hospital during the First World War. An unusual portrait of ex-President Clinton hangs in the hall.

ALUMNI SELECTION
Clement Attlee, William Beveridge, K.A. Busia, W.J. Clinton, Chelsea Clinton, Robert Dudley, Hugh Gaitskell, Paul Gambaccini, Max Hastings, Bob Hawke, Stephen Hawking, C.S. Lewis, John Radcliffe, Percy Byshe Shelley, Stephen Spender, Harold Wilson, Dornford Yates.

Chapel windows with serpent.

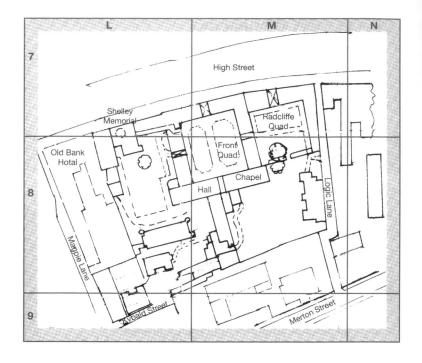

ALSO A LOCATION FOR
King Ralph 1991.

WADHAM COLLEGE

FOUNDED   1610 BY DOROTHY AND NICHOLAS WADHAM
OPEN TO PUBLIC   IN TERM TIME 1 – 4.15, IN VACATION 10.30 – 11.45
TEL 01865 277900 WWW.WADHAM.OX.AC.UK

Dorothy and Nicholas Wadham were Somerset landowners, Dorothy being the daughter of William Petre, re-founder of Exeter College. Until the Reformation, the site was an Augustinian Friary, then leased to citizens. Nicholas died in 1609. Dorothy sent her builder William Arnold but never came to Oxford herself. After the Restoration, the Royal Society started here. The college was low church and Whig. The chapel has glowing windows by Bernard Van Ling, but it and the Front Quadrangle are relatively stark. To the rear of the old quadrangle is a substantial and confusing array of modern buildings.

Always radical, the college has a reputation for activism, sometimes called 'The People's Republic of Wadham'. It has been said of Wadham students that even those who do nothing, do it with zest and enthusiasm.

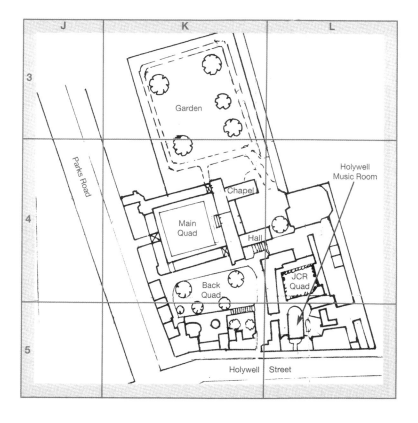

Nicholas and Dorothy
Wadham with James
I/VI over.

ALUMNI SELECTION

Monica Ale, Thomas Beecham, Melvin Bragg, Robert Boyle, Alan Bullock,
Michael Checkland, Cecil Day-Lewis, Michael Foot, C.B. Fry, Richard Ingrams,
Thomas Jackson, Felicity Jones, R.V. Jones, John Locke, Jodhe May, Firaz Khan
Noon, Johnson Hewlett, Frederick Lindemann, Lord Normanbrook, Rosamund
Pike, F.E. Smith, John Simon, Thomas Sprat, John Wilkins, John Wilmot,
Christopher Wren.

ALSO A LOCATION FOR

Dream Child 1985.

WORCESTER COLLEGE

FOUNDED	1714 SIR THOMAS COOKES (D.1701) AND GEORGE CLARKE
VISITORS	STRICTLY BY ARRANGEMENT

TEL 01865 278300 WWW.WORC.OX.AC.UK

On this site in 1283, Benedictines founded monastic Gloucester College for monks from its southern monasteries. After dissolution at the Reformation, in 1560 it became Gloucester Hall, guided by St John's College, and a Catholic retreat for such as the Catesbys, later involved in the Gunpowder Plot. The exhumed body of Amy Robsart, inconvenient wife of Robert Dudley, the Earl of Leicester, lay in the old hall for three days before burial in St Mary's. She is said to haunt the Junior Common Room. The will of Sir Thomas Cookes, a Worcestershire baronet, was contested but eventually Gloucester Hall benefited and it was renamed Worcester College.

Once through the rather dull college entry, the view is of a sunken lawn with grand 18th-century buildings on the north side and the 15th-century low monastic terrace on the other, through which passages lead to the garden. In 1790 the college sold land to allow the Oxford Canal to enter the city, possibly on the condition that it could have boat access, not realising that the canal would be at substantially higher level! Enough land was retained to form a sports field, making it the only college to have one integrally. The lake was formed in 1820

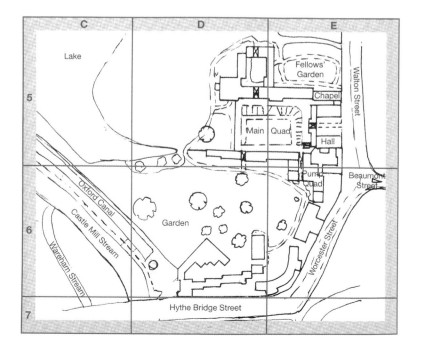

Front Quadrangle.

from a cattle-drinking area, and it drains under the canal to the Castle Mill Stream. The beautiful gardens were laid out in the English landscape style in 1827, and in them the first outdoor performance of *Alice in Wonderland* took place.

ALUMNI SELECTION
Richard Adams, Alistair Burnet, Thomas Caryat, William Catesby, Andy Green, Rupert Murdoch, John Sainsbury.

COLLEGES NOT FEATURED
IN THE MORSE FILMS

UNDERGRADUATE AND GRADUATE COLLEGES

Harris Manchester (M4) was founded in Manchester in 1786 for non-Anglicans. It was able to move to Oxford in 1889 after the 1871 religious reform. Financially stable due to the benefaction of a carpet magnate, Mr Harris, it added his name and became a full university college, for mature students, in 1996. There are spectacular pre-Raphaelite chapel windows by Edward Burne-Jones and William Morris. In 2003, seventy-six-year-old ex-high court judge Sir Oliver Popplewell joined the college as an undergraduate, so becoming the oldest student ever at Oxford. He says the academic standard is much higher than when he was at Cambridge in 1948.

    Tel 01865 271006 **Open to public** most weekdays

Jesus (J6) was founded in 1571 by Elizabeth I at the petition of Dr Hugh Price, Treasurer of St David's Cathedral, and is still known as 'The Welsh College'. It has a perfect Front Quadrangle and a dining hall with the most interesting paintings of any in Oxford. These include portraits of Elizabeth I by Nicholas Hilliard, and Dr Price, and Stuart Kings Charles I, by Van Dyke, and Charles II, probably because the college accommodated Royalist officers in the Civil War. Others include Harold Wilson, and T.E. Lawrence in his Arab clothes.

    Tel 01865 279700 **Open to public** 2 – 4 p.m.

Keble (J1) was founded in 1878 for poor men wishing to become clergymen, its founders involved with the Oxford Movement. It has distinctive Butterfield architecture in polychromatic brick, and a towering Gothic-revival chapel, which has never been consecrated. Holman Hunt's famous painting 'The Light of the World' is in a side chapel. The largest college in terms of student numbers, Keble has built a number of advanced 20th-century extensions.

    Tel 01865 272727 **Open to public** mainly p.m.

Lincoln (K7) was founded in 1427 by Richard Flemyng, Bishop of Winchester, to counter Lollardry. Its small 15th-century Front Quad contains a lawn of bowling-green quality, looked over by a bust of John Wesley and the Lincoln Imp, which reputably stops the buildings from collapsing.

    Tel 01865 279800 **Open to public** 2 – 5 for individuals

Mansfield (M2) was founded in 1886 for students from Free Churches and, like adjacent Manchester College, is designed in traditional college Gothic by Basil Champneys, in contrast to the nearby modern laboratories of the science area.

    Tel 01865 270999 **Open to public** by arrangement

The Queen's (N7) was founded in 1341 by Robert de Eglesfield, and chartered as a college in 1584. Originally taking students from the north of England, it developed arcane dining ceremonies. The main quadrangles were rebuilt between 1670–1760 in heavy classical style but with a baroque High Street façade. Nunn's Garden, reached by a walled alley to the left of the North Quad, creates a small charming contrast to the severity of the main buildings. The former celebrated college brewery is opposite.

Tel 01865 279120, **Open to public** 2 –5 by arrangement

St Catherine's (R2) was founded as a Society in 1962, but originated in 1868 when non-collegiate students were admitted, who founded in 1874 St Catherine's Club, to give financial assistance to students. No longer needed once the 1944 Education Act ensured funding, the Society became a college, with emphasis on science. Danish architect Arne Jacobsen designed the buildings on a rectilinear grid. Unlike most modern colleges, they are often visited. The design is meticulous, brilliant and also flawed: the front access is confused and the full-length bedroom windows cause occupants to drape various curtains for privacy and cooling. Oddities are a bell tower but no chapel, the first college not to have one, and the remains of Civil War earthworks in the gardens by the Holywell Mill Stream.

Tel 01865 271700 **Open to public** by arrangement

St Edmund Hall (N7) is a 13th-century academic hall that became a college in 1957, following a long subordinate association with neighboring The Queen's College. The Front Quad is charming, with a collection of buildings of the 17th to 20th centuries and a 13th-century well shaft. The church of St-Peter's-in-the-East (1130) was converted to the library in 1970, accessed through the yew trees of the graveyard. It has an atmospheric crypt below, the key for which can be obtained from the lodge.

Tel 01865 279005 **Open to public** daylight hours

St John's (H3) was founded in 1555 by Sir Thomas White, a merchant tailor. It is thought to be the wealthiest Oxford college, and to have the finest garden, which was laid out by Capability Brown. The old quadrangles are somewhat austere but there are varied modern extensions including the award-winning Garden Quad. This was Morse's college in the *Morse* novel *The Riddle of the Third Mile*.

Tel 01865 277300 **Open to public** 1 – 5

St Peter's (G7) was founded in 1928 by F.J. Chevasse, Bishop of Liverpool, and it became a full college in 1961. On the town side of Oxford, its mainly 19th–20th-century buildings include two former Canal Company offices. One with its cartouche of a narrow boat passing the Radcliffe Camera can be seen from the back garden, as can the castle mound and Nuffield College.

Tel 01865 278900 **Open to public** by arrangement

COLLEGES FOUNDED FOR WOMEN

As a result of the work of the Association for the Education of Women in Oxford, five colleges were established in the late 19th century. Most started in private houses and steadily developed from there. Their buildings are informal but, reflecting their period, not as untraditional as the later graduate colleges. They are set in pleasant gardens but their distance from the city centre invites few tourists or filmmakers.

Lady Margaret Hall (Norham Road) was founded in 1878 with strong Anglican connections and became co-educational in 1979. Modern brick buildings include Basil Champneys' Queen Anne-styled Wolfson Quad. The gardens lay alongside the Cherwell, with a punt inlet.

  Tel 01865 274300 **Open to public** by arrangement

St Anne's (Woodstock Road) was founded in 1879 and developed from the Society of Oxford Home Students. It admitted men in 1976.

  Tel 01865 274800 **Open to public** by arrangement

St Hilda's (Q11) was founded in 1893 by Dorothea Beale, and became a college in 1926. After much controversy, the college will admit men in 2008. The community of its women students enjoys a formidable reputation. Modern buildings include the Jacqueline Du Pré Music Room and the setting beside the Cherwell is exceptional.

  Tel 01865 276884 **Open to public** by arrangement

St Hugh's (St Margarets Road) was founded in 1886 by Elizabeth Wordsworth for four young poor women. It became a college in 1959 and admitted men in 1987. It has a large north Oxford garden.

  Tel 01865 274900 **Open to public** by arrangement

Somerville (G1) was founded in 1879. Its freedom from religious restraints perhaps led to it leading women's education and attracting free-thinkers, overseas students, scientists and trend-setters. It became a full college in 1951 and, although fiercely debated, admitted men in 1992. Somerville produced UK's first woman Prime Minister, Margaret Thatcher, a controversial Oxford figure.

  Tel 01865 270600 **Open to public** by arrangement

GRADUATE-ONLY COLLEGES

In the second half of the 20th century emphasis moved from teaching to research, especially in science, and seven colleges were founded mostly in the northern suburbs, their modern buildings reflecting their difference from the older formal colleges.

Linacre (N1) (South Parks Road) was founded in 1862 mainly for graduates from other universities and countries. It specialises in environmental studies.

  Tel. 01865 271650

t Antony's (Woodstock Road) was founded in 1953 by French Levantine ader Antonin Besse. It specialises in international relations.

Tel 01865 284700

Cross (H3) was founded in 1965 as a twin of Wolfson. It shares its site with Anglican seminary Pusey House. It is the most inaccessible of the central colleges but, inside, is charming.

Tel 01865 278490

Templeton (Kennington) was the Oxford Centre for Management Studies. It was renamed after a 1984 benefaction from ex-Rhodes scholar Sir John Templeton. With eighty graduates, most from overseas, it specialises in business management and is linked, by tutors in common and development policy, to the Saïd Business School, a university department. It hosts external government and business courses and conferences, in which students can become involved. It is the most remote college, occupying modern buildings south of Oxford.

Tel 01865 422500

Wolfson (Linton Road) was founded in 1965 as Iffley College, it changed its name after a grant from the Wolfson Foundation and became a college in 1981. Its reputation is egalitarian and non-hierarchical, and there are flats for families within its varied buildings designed by Powell and Moya. It is the fifth and most northerly college by the River Cherwell and a visitor straying off the riverside path will see an interesting garden and boat inlet.

Tel 01865 274100

COLLEGES NOT IN THE ABOVE CATEGORIES

All Souls College (L7) was founded in 1438 by Henry Chichele (Archbishop of Canterbury) and Henry VI as a chantry for the souls fallen in the 100 Years War with France, and to train priests to counter Lollardry. It remains the only old college that takes no students, and enjoys a high academic reputation. Original 15th-century buildings face the High Street. Behind and facing Radcliffe Square is Hawksmoor's 18th-century North Quad, over which the Morse cameras lingered, in views from the church tower.

Open to public occasionally 2 – 4, maximum group six

Tel 01865 279379 **www**.allsouls.ox.ac.uk

Kellogg (F3) was founded in 1990 from former Rewley House; it is Oxford's Open University, attracting part-time continuing education students, the numerical equivalent of three average colleges.

Tel 01865 270360

PERMANENT PRIVATE HALLS

From 1850, licensed Masters were permitted to open Private Halls, to provide low-cost Oxford education. In 1855 a statute established Permanent Private Halls; all that remain have their roots in religious movements.

CO-EDUCATIONAL

Regent's Park founded elsewhere in 1810 for Baptists, came to Oxford 1927, incorporated 1957.

120 students

Wycliffe Hall founded in 1877 for evangelists to counter Anglo-Catholicism.

Sixty-four students

RELIGIOUS ORDERS: THE FRIARIES WERE SUPPRESSED IN 1538

Blackfriars Dominicans, founded 1226, returned to Oxford 1929.

Thirty students

Campion Hall Society of Jesus founded in 1896 (Roman Catholics readmitted 1895).

Fourteen students

Greyfriars Franciscans (Capuchins) founded in 1224 re-established 1910.

Thirty-seven students

St Benets Hall Benedictines in Oxford from 1277, re-established Oxford 1899.

BUILDINGS OF THE UNIVERSITY
OF OXFORD

The **Ashmolean Museum** (H4) is the largest of the five university museums. It was originally in Broad Street and was based on the rarities of the Tradescent Collection, which after years of dispute finally fell to Elias Ashmole. The present building opened in 1845, designed in Greek revival style. The Old Ashmolean then became the History of Science Museum. The Ashmolean now has important collections of classical and modern art, artefacts, sculptures, a restaurant and shop. Among the exhibits is Cromwell's death mask, Guy Fawkes' lantern and Powhatan's Mantle. On the first floor is the Saxon Alfred's Jewel, its inscription translated as 'Alfred ordered me to be made'. It is believed to be part of a pointer to assist in reading English language bibles.

Open 10 – 5 Tuesday – Saturday, late opening Thursday in summer, 12 – 5 Sunday **Entry** free **Tel** 01865 278000 **www**.ashmol.ox.ac.uk

Bodleian Library (K5) was designed by Sir Giles Gilbert Scott in 1940. The central university library houses almost seven million books and documents, many rare. Books cannot be borrowed, so there are many reading rooms over the site. The building is undistinguished 'like a dinner suit made of Harris Tweed',

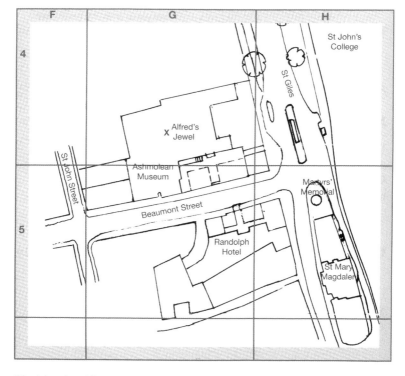

The Ashmolean Museum.

with five storeys below ground from which tunnels and conveyors service the other parts. Amongst many benefactions the library receives all royalties from Kenneth Graham's *The Wind in the Willows*. The library is open only to readers, and to groups led by Bodleian guides meeting at the Divinity School entrance.

Tel 01865 277224 **www**.bodley.ox.ac.uk

Botanic Garden (P8) The site is believed to have been the Jewish cemetery until 1290. In 1621 it became the Physic Garden for medical research, the third in Europe after Pisa and Leiden, and also linked botany, plant development and practical gardening. The London plane tree was developed here in 1665, and later the Oxford Ragwort, which escaped! Nicholas Stone built the great gateway in 1632. In 1840 the garden was finally renamed, and the emphasis shifted to science and evolution studies. There are several national plant collections here. The rose garden at the front was planted to commemorate the development of penicillin in 1935-40 by Howard Florey and team, with a memorial stone bearing their names. There are substantial hothouses near the Cherwell.

Open to public all year 9–5 (4.15 last entry). Apr – Aug. Guided walks can be arranged **Tel** 01865 286690 **www**.botanic-garden.ox.ac.uk

ALSO A LOCATION FOR

A seat near the river, facing into the garden, has become famous for being the meeting place of Lyra and Will in *The Amber Spyglass*, the last in the *His Dark Materials* trilogy by Philip Pullman.

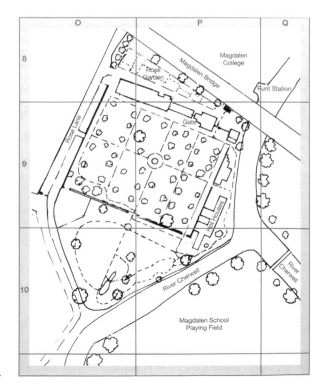

Botanic Garden.

The Clarendon Building (K5) was designed by Wren's pupil Nicholas Hawksmoor in 1713. Until 1826 it housed the University Press, founded in 1586, which preceded that situated in the University Church and Sheldonian Theatre. The building was named after its main benefactor, the Earl of Clarendon. His statue is at the west end. It is now part of the library and, apart from the central passage, not open to the public.

Holywell Music Room (M4) Built in 1748, this is reputedly the oldest extant music room in the world. It is administered by the Music faculty and Wadham College, has a capacity of 250, hosts popular musical events, coffee concerts and occasional lectures. The present layout is a restoration of its 18th-century design.
    Tel 01865 276125

Oxford Union (H6) is the political club of the university. It holds regular term-time debates, both serious and frivolous, and invites famous guest speakers. Oxford is politically powerful, having educated eight of the eleven British Prime Ministers since the Second World War (see below), although not all attended the Union. There is fierce competition to attain high office, which gives unrivalled opportunity to meet prominent figures. Public respect once shown to the students' debates, for example the King and Country Debate of 1933, has long gone as we have become less deferential, but the messages put over by guest speakers are often reported, for example when O.J. Simpson came after his trial in Los Angeles.

The Union started in 1825 and moved to its present site in 1852. The present Debating Chamber is from 1878, and all is in Gothic revival, in brick, unusually for Oxford. The old Debating Chamber has murals by members of the pre-Raphaelite group; photographs of visiting celebrities hang in the corridors and halls. The first woman to address members was a suffragette, the first woman president was in 1968, and the first overseas president was the American W.J. Bland in 1913, killed on the Western Front in 1918. Many students choose not to join the Union, believing it to be elitist, but it is becoming increasingly pop-oriented, for example when Kermit the Frog came to speak on frog and green matters.

The back garden is usually open for small quiet groups but ring 01865 241353 to ask for access to the buildings (www.oxford-union.org).

Prime Ministers educated at Oxford since the Second World War include: Clement Attlee, Anthony Eden, Alex Douglas-Hume, Harold Macmillan, Harold Wilson, Edward Heath, Margaret Thatcher and Tony Blair. Winston Churchill, Jim Callaghan and John Major did not attend university.

ALSO A LOCATION FOR
The Madness of King George 1994, *Oxford Blues* 1984. Opposite, in St Michael's Street, *Iris* 2001.

Oxford University Press (D1) Away from the great University institutions, in relatively humble Jericho, stands, in its imposing classical building, the fount of 'Oxford English'. The 'Press' started as a private company in the Sheldonian Theatre in 1672, built for itself the Clarendon Building in 1713, before moving to

Oxford University Press.

Walton Street in 1830. It has evolved into a University Department administered by Delegates drawn from senior scholars, with four divisions: Academic, UK Educational, Oxford Language Teaching and International (eleven overseas branches). Thirty per cent of its pre-tax surplus is donated to the university. Profits from Bible, Prayer Book and Dictionary publishing in the 18th and 19th centuries, as well as *The Oxford Book of English Verse* 1900, the first of the 'Oxford' books, have funded many university projects, for example the Ashmolean and Natural History Museums, and substantial one-off gifts continue to be made.

Pitt Rivers Museum (K1) This is one of the great ethnological museums of the world, based on the collection of Lt-Gen. Augustus Lane Fox Pitt Rivers. The building was completed *c.*1890 as an extension of the University Museum and is accessed through it.

    Open to public Monday – Saturday 12 – 4.30, Sunday 2 – 4.30
    Tel 270927 **www**.prm.ox.ac.uk

Radcliffe Infirmary Woodstock Road Oxford's oldest hospital took its first patients in 1770 and grew in importance until relieved in 1970 by the John Radcliffe Hospital (JR2) at Headington. It is now increasingly being used for university teaching, but the site is due for sale and redevelopment. Penicillin was demonstrated here as a vital drug in 1940. The first vessels used to grow the moulds were bedpans, later developed by Norman Heatley to become the 'penicillin bedpan' made in the Potteries. It is to be hoped that any site development will include a memorial to what is arguably Oxford's most important gift to the world.

Radcliffe Square (L6) is currently known as 'The heart of the University'. In the Middle Ages it was a mixed area of houses, taverns, apothecaries' workshops and academic halls. Catte Street is believed to have been the street of the rat-catchers. Exercising its control, the university cleared the area to form the square, dominated by James Gibbs' Radcliffe Camera, which is a reading room of the Bodleian Library and, unusually, a secular building with a dome. The north end of the square was excavated in 1912 to form deep book stacks. Tunnels and conveyors link to the main library. When part of the 1985 Spielberg film *Young Sherlock Holmes* was made in the square, the artificial snow that was used killed the open lawns around the Camera. After new turf was laid, railings were introduced. Four street lamps contain cameras linked to the police station. One street, at the corner of **Brasenose Lane**, still has a medieval central gutter. The east side of the square is dominated by Hawksmoor's grand north quad of All Souls College.

ALSO A LOCATION FOR
Young Sherlock Holmes 1985, *Opium Wars* 1996, *The Saint* 1997, *Red Violin* 1998, *Lawrence of Arabia* 2004.

St Mary the Virgin (L7) A church probably stood here at the east gate in the Saxon city wall, and development of the existing building began in the 11th century. It was consecrated in 1189, the north tower and steeple were added in the 13th century and the main rebuilding took place in the 15th and 16th centuries. Although administered by Oriel College, the university took over the building for ceremonies, meetings and its first library until the development of the Bodleian Library and the Sheldonian Theatre. Among the many incidents can be listed: 1357, the first penance paid by the town to the university for the attacks by the town boys on students. Payment continued for 550 years and marking the dominance of the university over the town; 1554-6, the trial of the Protestant Martyrs; 1560, burial, somewhere in the chancel, of Amy Robsart, inconvenient wife of Robert Dudley, Earl of Leicester; 1566 and 1592, visits by Elizabeth I; 1632, the High Street porch was the first classical construction in Oxford, its Catholic style caused religious controversy; 1642, after the Battle of Edgehill the head of the statue of the Virgin was shot off by Parliamentary troopers; 1642–6, Civil War burials; 1740s, John Wesley's sermons; 1833, the start of the Oxford Movement; 1940, the foundation of Oxfam.

The church has more visitors than many cathedrals and the best views over Oxford and area are from the tower, the steeple of which is 46m high.

    Open to public 9 – 5 (7 in summer) Tower £1.60 **Tel** 01865 279111 **www**.university-church.ox.ac.uk

Schools Quadrangle and Divinity School (K6) The Quadrangle was completed in 1624, in Gothic style, with the great Tower of the Five Orders on the east side with a statue of James I (VI Scotland), who took part in a library debate on the evils of tobacco as long ago as 1605. The lower rooms of the quadrangle were the first permanent university faculties. One now houses Thomas Bodley's exhibition room, occasionally open to the public. The statue of the 3rd Earl of Pembroke, Chancellor, is near the entrance to the Divinity School, which is accessed from the Schools Quad through the Proscholium. Work started on this in 1420 and was completed in 1490, with a magnificent English Perpendicular Gothic lierne vault. It is used in degree ceremonies, linking to the Sheldonian by Wren's door. Above it is Duke Humphrey's Library, sacked in the Reformation and the first to be revived by Bodley in 1602. A door in the west end leads to the Convocation House (1637) and the Chancellor's Court.

The area is usually open to the public 9 – 5 weekdays and 9 – 12 Saturdays except for ceremonies. The Convocation House and Duke Humphrey's Library are visited on the tours and very occasionally on open days.

Tel 01865 277000

ALSO A LOCATION FOR

The Hogwarts library was set in Duke Humphrey's Library in *Harry Potter and the Philosopher's Stone*, *The Saint* 1997, *Another Country* 1984, *To Kill a King* 2003, *Brideshead Revisited* TV series 1982.

Sheldonian Theatre (K5) was the first design in 1669 of Sir Christopher Wren, and the first classical Oxford structure, to replace the University Church as the ceremonial building of the university. It is based on the Roman Theatre of Marcellus, and judged by some as architecturally confused. Wren's technically advanced 21m-span roof was replaced in the 18th century, the painted ceiling is by Robert Streeter, the lantern 1828 by Blore. For their degree awards, students gather in the Divinity School and enter the Sheldonian through the end door. Honorary degree recipients first attend the Creweian Oration in the Vice-Chancellor's college and enter the side door. The Sheldonian is also used as a concert hall, not a conventional theatre. It is 'guarded' from Broad Street by a row of Herms or Emperors, remade 1972.

The building and quadrangle is open most weekdays and Saturday mornings, unless closed for ceremonies or concert rehearsals.

Open to public 10 – 12.30 2 – 4.30 **Entry** (to the building) £1.50
Tel 01865 277299 **www**.sheldon.ox.ac.uk

ALSO A LOCATION FOR

'Sweat runs down the emperors' brows at the sight of the beautiful Zuleika' *Zuleika Dobson* Max Beerbohm 1911, Wimsey proposes to Harriet Vane *Gaudy Night* Dorothy L. Sayers 1935.

The Oxford University Museum of Natural History (J1) The museum is housed in one of Oxford's outstanding buildings, completed in 1860 in distinctive Industrial Revolution Gothic, or French Baronial, style. Science at the university started here with the principle faculties housed in the building, which have gradually spread over the surrounding area. Special features are dinosaur skeletons and an imaginative but probably inaccurate reconstruction of a Dodo.

Open Mon – Sun 12 – 5 **Tel** 01865 272950 **www**.oum.ox.ac.uk

William Dunn School of Pathology (L1) became operational in 1927 after transfer of the subject from Christ Church to the University Museum. Great names associated with it include Sir Henry Acland, William Osler, George Dreyer and Howard Florey, who presided over the development of penicillin in the 1930s.

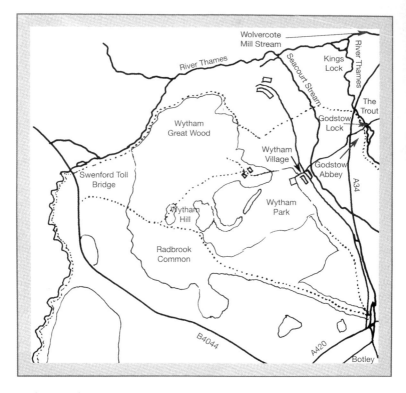

Wytham Woods.

Wytham Woods and Village The woods cover 900 acres and are owned and managed by the Oxford University for botanical and scientific research, for example analysing the effect on the food chain of micro-species. Wytham Hill, at 150m above sea level, is at the north end of a range of hills that diverts the Thames north, before again heading south-east past Oxford. Permits can be obtained from the university to visit the woods. Tel 01865 726832.

The village lies above the Seacourt Stream and is a pretty group of stone and thatched cottages with a classical village pub, The White Hart.

PART 4

A MORSE MISCELLANY

This part somewhat indulgently elaborates on a selection of the subjects touched on in the other parts. The *Statistical Summary* gives an overview of the old university for the statistically-minded, followed by a brief tribute to Anthony Minghella. In *The Importance of Morse* there is an attempt to analyse why people of all 'classes' across the world found something special in the *Morse* series. *The Music of Morse* gives proper recognition to composer Barrington Pheloung. *Town Vs Gown* gives the history of the troubles, although Morse's alleged criminals came from both sides but seldom attempted to reduce the other's population. *Oxford at War* offers an explanation of the survival of one of the icons of the series, the ancient buildings of the university. *Literary Oxford* places Colin Dexter in the firmament of graduate writers through the ages, for those who like lists. *Inspector Lewis* clears up many of the questions that must have been worrying keen Morse observers, but really the piece is included in the hope that a further TV series will be inspired by it! Finally *Extracts* is included for those who cannot be bothered to read the full text!

A STATISTICAL SUMMARY OF THE UNIVERSITY OF OXFORD

(Some figures are rounded up.)

There are thirty-nine, soon to be thirty-eight, independent colleges that join in a federation known as The University of Oxford.

Anyone who teaches, or is taught, is attached to a college and applies for admission to a college.

There are 20,000 students, and 8,000 staff employed by the university.

12,100 are undergraduates, 7,400 are postgraduates, plus additional students.

Thirty colleges admit both types of students, averaging 534 students.

Six to seven colleges admit only postgraduate students, averaging 319 students.

All Souls College takes no students; Kellogg College is for continuing education.

6,900 students come from outside the UK.

Twenty-three per cent of students made successful applications, and applied to colleges that have tutors in their chosen subject.

Forty-seven per cent of the students are female; all colleges will be co-educational by October 2008.

The university administers the subject faculties, the Bodleian Library, five museums, the Botanic Garden, Oxford University Press, substantial properties and sets the examinations and awards the degrees.

Colleges are charities and do not publish full accounts.

Grotesques are a feature of Gothic buildings. If they drain rainwater, they are gargoyles.

ANTHONY MINGHELLA

6th January 1954–18th March 2008

It was in 1985, ten years after his first novel was published, that Colin Dexter received a life-changing call. Could a Central TV producer, Kenny McBain, come down to Oxford to talk to him about the possibility of adapting one, perhaps two, of his *Morse* stories for the small screen? The delegation that arrived also included Julian Mitchell and the relatively unknown Anthony Minghella. Unaware of the protocol, the author wondered how much he would have to pay them, but was pleased to learn that it was the opposite. He offered to accompany them around the locations of his books, but they said they had already done that. Minghella already knew which would be the first adaptation – not the first book but the fifth, *The Dead of Jericho*, and so the character of Morse was created by John Thaw, Minghella and Colin Dexter. DS Lewis, middle-aged in the books, was re-cast as a younger man, at first at odds with and baffled by the mercurial Inspector. What emerged was a classic crime story, full of clearly defined characters and events, that has held its place as one of the best of all the *Morse* episodes.

THE IMPORTANCE OF MORSE

Every week of the year a *Morse* tour leaves the Tourist Information Centre. In the summer three or four guides are employed and visitors, from all over the world, sometimes have to be turned away. Several years after the last *Morse* film was made there is no apparent reduction in interest. Despite the Oxford connections of authors such as Lewis Carroll, J.R.R. Tolkien, C.S. Lewis, none have created quite such interest. It is possible to explain this phenomenon by referring to the power of popular television, by the sheer volume of episodes, by the use of Oxford as a backdrop, but only partly.

Is the explanation that *Morse* tuned in to the end of the period of deference, when the public was no longer prepared to buy into the myth of Oxford, or many other myths for that matter? From the time of Chaucer and Shakespeare, through the period of the 18th-century poets, to when Lewis Carroll sat in his 'ivory tower' of Christ Church, one side of the city, the university, had been praised and revered. And just as, for example, canal boats became more decorated as the economics of canal trade collapsed, or Gothic architecture became more elaborate as it gave way to modern styles, so, as the university declined, the chorus of praise for it grew louder. The cavorting of the young men of *Brideshead*, as they waited for another war, looks foolish now. When, in 1933, students voted at the Oxford Union not to fight for King and Country, the nation was shocked; today they would be ignored, as it seems they only get noticed when they invite a controversial speaker to address them.

After so much sweetness, the public was ready for some sour, and Dexter and the screenwriters gave it to them. At last, we were seeing academics with feet of clay, tormented students and a rounded, if somewhat middle class, town, whose inhabitants were just as imperfect. Surveying them cynically was an improbable, sensitive, intuitive policeman, who could not fight, limped (John Thaw had childhood polio), and often got things wrong, and his admiring, often baffled, down-to-earth Sergeant.

Morse is now an historical series and, in many ways, always was. It bridges the gap between the amateur sleuths of Conan Doyle and Agatha Christie and the gritty, technology-driven detectives of modern police dramas (the rural *Midsomer Murders*, often filmed in local villages, being a notable exception). Morse could no more operate in today's world than he could freely drive his Jaguar around Oxford's streets. As such he is a link between the old, comfortable (for some) world, and today's uncertainties.

THE MUSIC OF MORSE

Most notable films have memorable music and the *Morse* series is no exception. Australian musician Barrington Pheloung composed distinctive scores for each episode and the signature tune features the rhythm of the Morse code. This was a musical pun, because the detectives were named after Fellow crossword enthusiasts of Colin Dexter.

The music often echoes the classical tastes of the fictional Morse, and of John Thaw and Colin Dexter, judging by their choice of recordings when each became castaways on Radio 4's *Desert Island Discs*. When appropriate, other styles were used, e.g. R&B in *Who Killed Harry Field?* and Country and Western in *Promised Land*, both probably more to Lewis's taste! *The Wench is Dead* is greatly enhanced by its atmospheric skirling music.

The composer was conducting a choir in Exeter College chapel singing the *Te Deum* from Faure's *Requiem* (a Dexter choice) when Morse collapsed outside. A CD of the Morse collection has been recorded.

Some believe the killer's name in an appropriate episode can be heard in code; Samuel Morse 1791-1872 would have been intrigued. For readers who wish to test this theory, the Morse code is given below.

A •−   B −•••   C −•−   D −••   E •   F ••−•   G −−•   H ••••
I ••   J •−−−   K −•−   L •−••   M −−   N −•   O −−−   P •−−•
Q −−•−   R •−•   S •••   T −   U ••−   V •••−   W •−−   X −••−   Y −•−−   Z −−••

TOWN VS GOWN

The 700-year-long, at times bitter, contest for control of Oxford, between the 'Town' and its university, the 'Gown', has always interested visitors. Perhaps the two rhyming words tease the imagination, or perhaps it is difficult to comprehend how this fair city could ever have been the scene of such bloody rivalry. Today the two sides live comfortably together, as they probably did in the early days, when a few scholars drifted into Oxford. In between, there is a well-documented history of dispute and mayhem, although how much it impacted on everyday life is uncertain.

Many of the underlying causes are certainly known. In the early Middle Ages, the town was already a flourishing commercial centre, not delighted to be invaded by young, often poor, anti-social students, speaking in alien Latin, which proclaimed their difference and superiority. In 1209 a student killed a townswoman with an arrow and in retaliation two students were hung. The rest fled, some to Cambridge where there was probably a small university, and, for five years, Oxford's university was suspended. Throughout the 13th century, starting with Dominicans in 1221, often aggressive friars established houses in Oxford to combat heresy and urbanism. Development brought in tradesmen of all types, not all willing to respect the local community. Outlaws found it easy to infiltrate into the chaotic population. Price controls in favour of the university aroused strong resistance. Students, half of whose possessions were weapons, divided into North and South and fought what is known as the Nations Riots. Most of the in-comers were men, so unlike most of the country, Oxford was predominately a testosterone-driven male community, and this continued until late into the 20th century.

In the turbulent plague- and famine-ridden 14th century, there was strong anti-clerical feeling, manifested nationwide in attacks on many abbeys and cathedrals. The university was perceived as part of the Church, subject only to internal discipline, although students were among those who stormed the important nearby Abingdon Abbey. John Wyclif's Lollards caused dissension within and outside the university. Alcohol fuelled the underlying resentment felt by those without power, wealth, education and privilege against strangers who had them, and who, furthermore, were always supported in any dispute by Crown and Church.

Hostilities continued long after the Reformation had reduced the power and wealth of the Church. Until 1825, the Mayor and sixty-two townsmen had to pay a penance at the University Church for sixty-three students killed by townspeople in the great St Scholastica's Riot of 1355. In the 17th-century Civil War, the university supported the occupying Royalists, the Town sided with Parliament. Political and economic differences, such as Jacobinism in the early 18th century, began to replace religious ones. An exception was in 1798, when Town and Gown together formed a Volunteer Force to repel possible invasion from French and American revolutionaries. The Oxford Medical School's insatiable demand for bodies in the 18th and 19th centuries, often employing grave-robbers and body-snatchers and dumping the remains in the castle ditch, could not have helped relations. Frequent targets of the mob were Methodists,

Baptists, Quakers and other non-conformists. In the 19th century, there was resistance to the university-led Oxford Movement, and a public appeal raised finance for the construction of the Martyrs' Memorial, to act as a reminder of the days of religious intolerance. This was also the golden age of the upper-class public school students known as the 'Hearties', whose primary interest was in sport of all kinds, including Town-baiting.

Alcohol, social inequalities and the innate belligerence of the British continued to fuel unrest into the 20th century. However, as the university gradually lost its special privileges, hostilities died, and although Guy Fawkes Night became a traditional excuse for student excesses, townspeople learnt to keep away. Student discipline continued to be administered by the recently disbanded Bulldogs, the university's police headed by the Marshal. By 1960, after at least 760 years of conflict, the two sides settled into their present harmony with the advent of universal education, stricter civil policing, the mellowing effect of an increasing number of women students, a less class-ridden, more mature, university, and the distractions of computers and mass entertainment.

Of the many events that mark the conciliation between the two ancient rivals, two in particular can be singled out. In the first half of the 20th century, it is estimated that £27m was gifted to the university by William Morris from the profits of his Morris Motors car company. He later became Lord Nuffield, and the company is now German-owned. At the end of the century, car traffic was diverted by the City Council away from the university area, to the detriment of the Town area. To partially compensate, the Town usually beats the university in the many sporting fixtures now organised between the two sides.

Town.   Gown.

OXFORD AT WAR

Visitors are often intrigued to observe how little mark a millennium of conflict has left on Oxford's ancient buildings (not all of which are as old as they look). A brief summary of what is left, and of what has been destroyed, is as follows:

850–1060   Viking raids: the earth and timber wall has gone, but it set the north and south lines of the later stone wall.

1142   Siege of Oxford: the descendants of the Conqueror, Stephen of Blois and Empress Matilda, fought for the throne. The stone wall still standing on the south and north-east of the old city, and the castle, would have existed. Matilda escaped from the siege to Wallingford.

1337–1453   100 Years War with France. All Souls College founded as memorial to all those who died 1438.

1455–1485   Wars of the Roses. Magdalen College founded 1458.

1642–1646   Civil War. Oxford occupied by Royalists after the Battle of Edgehill. A massive earth defence thrown up well outside of the line of the 12th-century wall, some traces remain. Royalist graves exist in the University Church. The porch of the church, seen as a Roman Catholic symbol, caused great controversy. The Corn Market lead roof was stripped for bullet manufacture, leading to its removal. Fire destroyed the buildings on the Town side of Cornmarket. Magdalen tower used as a lookout as Parliamentary besiegers surrounded the city. No fighting took place in the city, but outposts destroyed. Profits from Lord Clarendon's *History of the Great Rebellion* helped fund construction of Hawksmoor's Clarendon Building 1711-13. A number of paintings and statues exist of Charles I and Henrietta Maria. Substantial iconoclasm after the war by the Puritans.

1899–1902   Boer War. Cecil Rhodes, died 1902, founded Rhodes Scholarships from 1903.

1914–1918   First World War Oxford again became a garrison town. Colleges accommodated army and aeronautical cadets. The Examination School, High Street, became the Third Southern Regional Hospital. A former operating theatre can be seen in the basement; bodies were taken out of the back into Merton Street. Officially 2,708 students and graduates were killed; their memorials stand in every college. Sixteen VCs were won. Every name represents family tragedy and national loss. One who survived, T.E. Lawrence, is remembered by paintings and sculptures in Jesus College and All Souls College. His relatively insignificant successes against the Turks in Arabia coincided with the disaster of Gallipoli, promoting him to a national, if reluctant, hero. Gertrude Bell, a graduate of Lady Margaret Hall, was also in the Arab Bureau and was involved in setting the borders of modern Iraq. Vera Brittain, mother of Shirley Williams, lost her brother and fiancé on the Western Front, and wrote the poignant *Testament of Youth*.

1939–1945   Second World War. Some 15,000 evacuees and several government departments came to Oxford, more might have come if it had been known that no bombs would fall on it! The reasons for this are obscure: there was a pact between Oxford, Cambridge and Heidelburg, and there was no industry, excluding the car works at Cowley, which produced tanks, cartridge cases and repaired Hurricanes. A popular theory is that Oxford was earmarked as a future capital. Central Oxford's output was not inconsiderable. Development of penicillin, research on which began in the university science area early in the 1930s, continued to its important conclusion. Academics and printers produced propaganda. Academics went to Bletchley Park to crack the Enigma code, photo-reconnaissance analysis took place at Kidlington. Oxfam started in 1942. Magdalen College saved their ancient deer herd from the Ministry of Food by a sophisticated argument that, as deer are herbivores, they were in fact vegetables! Although fewer students perished compared to during the First World War, there was substantial loss, for example the winning eight of Trinity College boat crew lost all but two of its members.

LITERARY OXFORD

Below is a random list of some of the most celebrated writers who were educated at Oxford. Dates roughly reflect the writers' Oxford period.

14TH CENTURY
Wycliffe John (Balliol)

16TH CENTURY
More Thomas (Oriel)
Raleigh Walter (Oriel)
Sydney Phillip (Christ Church)
Tyndale William (Hertford)

17TH CENTURY
Aubrey John (Trinity)
Burton Robert (Christ Church)
Clarendon E.H. (Magdalen Hall)
Donne John (Hertford)
Locke John (Christ Church)
Wood Anthony (Merton)

18TH CENTURY
Evelyn John (Trinity)
Gibbon Edward (Magdalen)
Johnson Samuel (Pembroke)
Wesley Charles (Christ Church)
Wesley John (Christ Church)

19TH CENTURY
Arnold Matthew (Oriel)
Beerbohm Max (Merton)
Blackmore R.D. (Exeter)
Bridges Robert (Corpus Christi)
Burton Richard (Trinity)
Carroll Lewis (Christ Church)
De Quincey Thomas (Worcester)
Hopkins Gerard Manley (Balliol)
Housman A.E. (St John's)
Hughes Thomas (Oriel)
Morris William (Exeter)
Murray James (Hon MA D.Litt)
Newman J.H. (Oriel-Trinity)
Pater Walter (Brasenose)
Ruskin John (Christ Church)
Shelley Percy Byshe (University)
Southey Robert (Balliol)

Swift Jonathon (Hertford)
White Gilbert (Exeter)
Wilde Oscar (Magdalen)

20TH CENTURY
1900-50
Amis Kingsley (St Johns)
Auden W.H. (Christ Church)
Awdry W.H. (St Peters)
Beadle Muriel (Balliol)
Belloc Hillaire (Balliol)
Betjeman John (Magdalen)
Brittain Vera (Somerville)
Buchan John (Brasenose)
Crispin Edmund (St John's)
Day-Lewis Cecil (Wadham)
Eliot T.S. (Merton)
Galsworthy John (New College)
Giesel Theodor Seuss (Lincoln)
Golding William (Brasenose)
Grahame Kenneth (St Edwards Schl)
Graves Robert (St John's)
Greene Graham (Balliol)
Herbert A.P. (New College)
Hillary Richard (O.A.T.C.)
Holtby Winifred (Somerville)
Huxley Aldous (Balliol)
Huxley Julian (Balliol)
Innes Michael (Oriel)
Larkin Philip (St John's)
Lawrence T.E. (Jesus-All Souls)
Lees-Milne J. (Magdalen)
Lewis C.S. (Magdalen)
Longford Elizabeth (L.M.H.)
MacKenzie Compton (Magdalen)
MacNiece Louis (Merton)
McCauley Rose (Somerville)
Milne A.A. (St Catherine's)
Mitchison Naomi (St Anne's)
Murdoch Iris (Somerville)
Naipaul V.S. (Balliol)
Novello Ivor (Magdalen)

Pym Barbara (St Hilda's)
Rattigan Terence (Trinity)
Renault Mary (St Hugh's)
Sayers Dorothy L. (Somerville)
Scott C.P. (Corpus Christi)
Spender Stephen (University)
Tolkien J.R.R. (Merton)
Toynbee Arnold (Balliol)
Waugh Evelyn (Hertford)
Yates Dornford (University)

1950–21ST CENTURY
Adams Richard (Worcester)
Amis Martin (Exeter)
Atkins Peter (Lincoln)
Bennett Alan (Exeter)
Berners-Lee Tim (The Queen's)
Bragg Melvyn (Wadham)
Brown Tina (Exeter)
Bullock Alan (St Cats – New Col)
Carpenter Humphrey (Keble)
Churchill Carol (Lady Margaret Hall)
Clark Alan (Christ Church)
Currie Edwina (St Anne's)
Dawkins Richard (New College)
Dexter Colin (Cambridge)
Fielding Helen (St Anne's)
Forster Margaret (Somerville)
Fowles John (New College)
Fraser Antonia (L.M.H.)
Greenfield Susan (Lincoln-St Hilda's)
Haddon Mark (Merton)

Hawking Stephen (University)
Hibbert Christopher (Oriel)
Hislop Ian (Magdalen)
Ingrams Richard (University)
Innes Michael (Oriel)
Jenkins Roy (Balliol)
Kingston Miles (Trinity)
Lancaster Osbert (Lincoln)
Le Carre John (Lincoln)
Lively Penelope (St Anne's)
Marks Howard (Balliol)
Mitchell Julian (Wadham)
Mitchison Naomi (St Anne's)
Mortimer John (Brasenose)
Motion Andrew (University)
Murdoch Rupert (Worcester)
Murray James (Corpus Christi)
Omaar Rageh (New College)
Palin Michael (Brasenose)
Pears Iain (Wadham)
Potter Dennis (New College)
Pullman Philip (Exeter)
Rantzen Esther (St Anne's)
Stein Rick (New College)
Taylor A.J.P. (Magdalen)
Thomas Rosie (St Hilda's)
Tynan Ken (Magdalen)
Wain John (St John's)
Waugh Auberon (Christ Church)
Winterson Jeanette (Somerville)
Wright Peter (St Peter's)

INSPECTOR LEWIS

This spoof chapter was written for the first edition (2003), before there was any talk of a Lewis series!

At his desk in 2004, Lewis gloomily considered the mundane crimes on his files, nothing but family rows and road rages. Once more his thoughts turned to the reason why all the interesting crimes stopped with the death, four years ago, of his old boss Morse. Lewis had hoped for so much more on his promotion, but since it, he had not visited even one college. Before, he was always in one or the other of them; bodies lay all over the university, those were great days. Admittedly most of the people they had arrested were never prosecuted, due to lack of evidence, and even the clever ones seemed confused at what had happened, but the cases were really interesting and the crimes seemed to follow Morse around.

His mind went back over the cases he and Morse had shared. First of all, there was the mystery of the small quiet man who often seemed to be near the crime scene, often in disguise, who uncharacteristically Morse did not seem to notice. Sometimes he was in a college wearing a gown, sometimes a librarian, a chorister, a drunk, even a tramp. Go into a pub, there he was in the corner. Morse was often seen exchanging glances with him. Lewis had heard that the man had been known to boast at private meetings that he had actually devised the crimes, there was no proof, but could it be true?

Take a few of the old cases, such as when he first met Morse climbing out of Anne Staveley's cottage after having broken in, and who really killed George Jackson? Then in case 2, Morse had got very excited at meeting his crossword tormenter Daedalus, the next moment Daedalus was dead. In case 3, did Harry Josephs attack Morse on the church tower or was it the other way round, before he, Lewis, fatally intervened? In case 10, Morse tried to prove that Anthony Donn, who seemed to know Morse from the past, had been killed by his wife Kate, but how could she have got into the college, and where was Morse when the customs officer was killed in the cricket pavilion. Not in his deckchair, Lewis was sure. Another who knew Morse from the past, Sir Alexander Reece, also did not last long. In case 28 why had Morse insisted that they came away from a murder investigation to see that opera singer receive a degree and why was he so horrified when she was shot? It was obvious that Victor Ignotas had not shot her from a reading room, so who was on the roof? How was Morse so sure, in case 29, that Karen Andersen was in Wytham Woods, with no evidence whatsoever? Who had put the ones they called The Daughters of Cain up to such a cunning crime, after Morse had taken a key suspect punting on the Cherwell? And finally what was going on between Morse and the Harrisons in his last case?

The more Lewis thought about it, the more he realised that it could not all have been coincidental. If he were ever to make Chief Inspector, he would have to comb Oxford until he found Morse's old accomplice!

EXTRACTS AND QUOTATIONS

'*Morse liked nothing more than fingering the collar of his social superiors*'

'*… thought why there wasn't more blood or were you just grateful?* Morse: '*I was grateful*'

'*that superannuated policeman, with that scrapheap of a car*'

'*the villainous Charles Franks would not have got away with it if Morse had been around*'

'*Sophocles would be surprised to find himself prominent in a 20th-century police series*'

'*to about 30 men and 11 women who committed unnecessarily interesting crimes and demanded so little proof before giving themselves up*'

'*Professor Drysdale murders Ballarat and dumps him (limbless) in the canal, Reece murders Kerridge, Drysdale shoots Reece. An everyday story of university folk*'

'*the bursar was only a mild pornographer and adulterer, really quite normal*'

'*it also assumes that good-looking young women are likely to fight for the attention of an elderly male academic*'

'*one 16th-century Principal, Alexander Nowell, accidentally invented bottled beer but surprisingly has been given no memorial*'

'*James Bond has a Danish lesson, advancing the cause of the one-to-one tutorial before being interrupted*'

'*Cornford runs through Brasenose College gatehouse and into Oriel College*'

'*the Union is becoming increasingly pop-orientated, for example when Kermit the Frog came to speak on frog and green matters*'

'* a healthy proportion of students find it easy to ignore BNC's proximity to the Bodleian Library*'

'*did the college fellows realise how they would be caricatured when they took the location fees and will they ever take the same risk again?*'

'*I shall treasure the guide and I hope that may others will do the same*' Colin Dexter

'*I hope you have a big success with it*' Philip Pullman

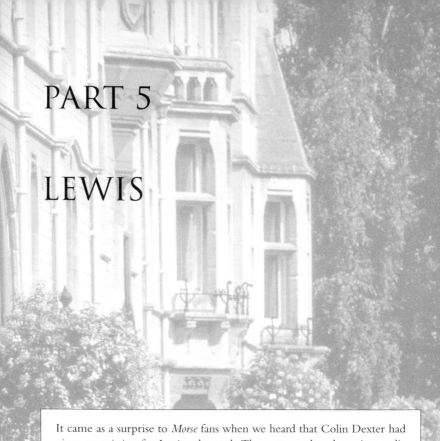

PART 5

LEWIS

It came as a surprise to *Morse* fans when we heard that Colin Dexter had given permission for *Lewis* to be made. The news produced massive media interest, with even the BBC promoting the pilot episode, although it was to be made by ITV. Permission was given on two conditions; firstly, that Kevin Whately reprised his role, and secondly that it was to be based in Oxford.

For the same production team that made Morse, the prospect was both appealing and daunting. Morse was an unlikely and intriguing character, and John Thaw was a charismatic actor. Lewis was always in his shadow, a pragmatic and rather dull family man. Whereas Morse had many likes (alcohol, pubs, crosswords, Wagner and 'real music', choral singing, divas, his Jaguar, young women, intuition, Lewis) and dislikes (heights, corpses, paperwork, exercise, technology, superiors (especially academics), religion, the honours system and the tabloid press), Lewis had few of either. He liked his family, egg and chips, playing by the rules, technology, cricket, tunes and Morse (although not always). This was hardly the stuff of heroes.

Then there was the problem of explaining what had happened in the five years since Morse had died. Had the spate of murders in Oxford magically stopped, and if not, who had been solving them? Could Lewis be transformed into a romantic sleuth? How to replace Superintendent Strange (James Grout was too ill to come back, and in any case was near to retirement at the end of *Morse*) and the Jaguar car? The pilot would be crucial.

Claire Holman reappeared as the pathologist Dr Laura Hobson, having clearly not made a career move (unlikely; nobody stays in Oxford that long!) and the policy was for Oxford itself to be the icon, replacing the Jaguar.

REPUTATIONS

PILOT	29TH JANUARY 2006
DIRECTOR	BILL ANDERSON
WRITER	STEPHEN CHURCHETT
STORY	RUSSELL LEWIS

SUMMARY

We are introduced to two new regular characters. Taking Lewis's old position is DS Hathaway (Laurence Fox), the mirror image of the Morse-Lewis partnership. Hathaway is university educated (Cambridge), cultured and clearly on the fast track. Strange has been replaced by a woman, Chief Superintendent Jean Innocent (Rebecca Front).

Lewis's absence is explained by an overseas training posting, taken after his wife was killed in a hit-and-run accident, presumably to clear the way for future romantic interest. His children have dispersed; the slate has been wiped clean. Met by Hathaway at Heathrow, he wears an un-Lewis-like exotic shirt that does not match his expression. He is then almost knocked over by a maroon Jaguar; shades of Morse keep appearing. Lewis is grumpy throughout the episode, especially after his meeting with his new boss.

However, he soon has three murders, two suicides (one mysteriously unsuccessful) and an old unsolved death in a car crash to cheer him up. Rapidly he has to come to terms with modern devices that would have driven his old boss to the nearest hostelry – CCTV, e-mail, keypads, mobiles and text messaging, laptops, answer phones, video diaries, types of oars, women superiors, and the mathematical conundrums of Perfect Numbers and Goldbach Conjecture. Hoodies, much in the news at the time, were regulation wear for the criminals, and protective overalls for the detectives (not Morse's style)!

To make him feel more at home, there is the usual maniacal, dysfunctional family in the big house; this time the Griffon family with a sports car. They are a little upset because the previous owner, Johnny, had died in Morse's time in his Griffon, after being told that his son Danny was not his child, but employee Tom Pollock's. Danny believes Johnny's younger twin Rex murdered his father (he did not) and is selling the firm out to a Japanese company before he can inherit (he is). Pollock's daughter, Jessica, loves Danny, who is a student at Oxford, not realizing he is her half-brother. Pollock is shot in the shower. The mother, Trudi, sees a hooded figure fleeing and assumes it is Danny, who wears a hoodie. Rex naturally puts Pollock's body in his car boot and leaves it in Oxford Station's car park, and immediately the car is stolen by three hoodies, who get caught. Danny's body is found in a rowing skiff. Jessica walks into the Thames at the same spot, but is rescued. Both Rex and Danny had a relationship with Regan Peverill, the first victim at the Pretorius Laing Institute.

Despite the sub-plots, the crime was about the Goldbach Conjecture. Student Regan is a mathematical genius, Danny is not, but they both know too much. Morse keeps coming back, and there is a hint of there having been a meaningful relationship between him and Trudi. Hathaway opts to work with Lewis. Will

Kate trap Lewis, or go the way of all of Morse's squeezes?
   Is the stage set for a series?

OXFORD LOCATIONS

Wadham College Danny Griffon's room; Denniston's seminar; garden walk (the astrolabe is a prop!). A bowler-hatted Colin Dexter points their way to Danny's room.

Oriel Square and College (Island Quad) Jessica competes for the Endeavour Music award (the building colours have changed since).

River Thames, Port Meadow Danny rows, shoots, and is found dead in a skiff: Jessica wades in.

River Thames, College boat house discussion on various types of oars. Jessica walks just below Folly Bridge.

River Thames, Trout Inn, Wolvercote Lewis and Hathaway go for celebratory drink (just like old times).

Magdalen Bridge and Botanic Garden Lewis receives lolly from Kate Jekyll, then begins to understand the notes Morse had left.

St Giles where DI Knox, Hathaway's boss, is breathalysed, letting Lewis in on the case.

City views Martyrs' Memorial and Randolph Hotel, Radcliffe Square, Hertford; All Souls and Trinity Colleges, Broad Street.

OUTSIDE OXFORD

Gaddesdon Place, Hemel Hempstead, Herts the Griffon home.

Pretorious Laing Institute Experimental Techniques Centre, Brunel University, Uxbridge, Middlesex. Interiors at the old DSS office, The Mall, Ealing.

The airport Terminal 4, Heathrow Airport.

Station car park West Car Park, Brunel Way, Slough Railway Station.

Ivor Denniston's House Woodville Gardens, Ealing, West London.

The churchyard St Laurence's Church, Church Road, Cowley, Uxbridge.

The Mortuary St Peter's Hospital, Chertsey Hospital.

Police Station TAVR Centre, Honeycroft Hill, Uxbridge.

The supermarket Sainsbury's, The Dome, North Western Road, North London.

The Pathology Laboratory Northwick Park Hospital, Harrow, Middlesex.

The car park Fox Wood C.P., Hillcrest Road, Ealing.

1 WHOM THE GODS WOULD DESTROY

SERIES 1   18TH FEBRUARY 2007
WRITER   DANIEL BOYLE
DIRECTOR   MARC JOBST

SUMMARY

In their youth four former Oxford students – Linn, Platt, Greeley and Bundrick – formed a Bacchalanian society based on drugs, excess and the God Dionysus, and called themselves 'The Sons of the Twice Born'. Linn is in line for becoming the head of the university, Bundrick has a bicycle shop, Platt is wheelchair-bound after a road accident and Greeley is a bad artist. During a meeting on Platt's estate they kill a prostitute and now her daughter, Ann, and two other women, calling themselves the Furies, are belatedly out for revenge and searching to find out where the body is buried.

Morse would have sorted this out in no time at all, and Hathaway, with his classical education, should have picked up on the Furies' motivation, but Lewis is, with the average viewer, understandably baffled for most of the episode. The Furies are rocking, the Sons are rolling, and it is an overwhelming 4–0 win. Linn kills Greeley, Bundrick kills Linn and is arrested, while Platt is savaged by his wife Ann's hounds, she being a Fury. Her mother's body is (guess where): by the statue of Dionysus. Lewis's sympathies are with the Furies and he decides to bring no charges, to the detriment of the local police clear-up rate.

OXFORD LOCATIONS

Magdalen College opening scenes; Linn's college; up steps towards Hall; plays answerphone call from a Fury; see oil leaks from Linn's car similar to those near Greeley's body.

Oriel College the dining hall.

New College concert; Lewis stares out Linn.

New College Lane Lewis pursues Linn, somehow loses him.

Duke Humphrey's, Bodleian Library Lewis interviews Professor Cole about the 'Sons'.

Turl Street Lewis and Dr Hobson meet.

Radcliffe Square and Camera and Brasenose Lane Brasenose College; call on Linn.

Oxford railway station Ingrid Nielson arrives.

St Giles and Randolph Hotel Lewis walks into hotel and tells Ingrid of her husband Greeley's death.

Bike Zone, Market Street Bundrick's bicycle shop; Bundrick finds note from a Fury. Bundrick arrested.

Lewis. (Courtsey ITV plc)

Ashmolean Museum Hathaway instructs Lewis about Greek mythology.
Medical Sciences Teaching Centre, South Parks Road laboratory
Sheldonian Quad and Theatre Lewis walks with Professor Cole; Lewis
disagrees with Hathaway.

OTHER LOCATIONS

Greeley's narrow boat River Thames, Shiplake College, near Henley. Greeley
murdered on river bank.
Theodore Platt's house Allanbay Park Estate, How Lane, Binfield, Berks.
Theodore Platt's grounds with temple; grave of Patsy Worth West Wycombe
Park, High Wycombe, Bucks.
Linn's hideaway cottage Druids Cottage, Round House and Tower Ridge
Farm, West Wycombe Park.
Crime scene Hellbottom Wood, West Wycombe Park.
Police Station; University Society Archives; interior Love Lines; Morgue
QinetiQ building, 124 Chobham Lane, Longcross, Chertsey, Surrey.
Lewis's house Flat 2, 10 Gordon Road, Ealing, London.
Pub the Cricketers, Housellbirch, Housell, Woking, Surrey.
Hospital interior Ward 3, Ravenscourt Hospital, Chiswick, London: after Platt's
home-operation.
Crypt, where the 'Sons' meet, Hathaway overhears St Mary Magdalene
Church, Rowington Close, Paddington, London.
Dental practice interior: The Ealing D.P., 6 Drayton Green Road, West Ealing,
London.
Love Lines 69 Askew Road, London W12: Hathaway rings: voice syncronisation.
Car parked for observation Becklow Road, W12.
Coffee Shop, Ingrid Neilson The Foresters, 2 Leighton Road, Ealing, London.
Tina Daniel's flat 66 Sherwood Close, West Ealing.

2 OLD SCHOOL TIES

SERIES 1   25TH FEBRUARY 2007
WRITER   ALAN PLATER
DIRECTOR   SARAH HARDING

SUMMARY

Our heroes are assigned to bodyguard a celebrity author, Turnbull, who is invited to speak at the Oxford Union. He is a reformed computer-hacker who defrauded organisations, including two Oxford colleges, and has received death threats. The Union's reception committee consists of two amoral women students and two men, one an ex-rugby international, David Harvey.

One of the women is strangled in the room next to that in which Turnbull has entertained the other one. After confiding that the death threats are a publicity stunt, Turnbull is shot. It transpires that Harvey's father was bursar of one of the colleges Turnbull had swindled, and as a result committed suicide. Harvey had planned revenge with the women, but when that failed he hired a hitman.

A shoal of red herrings swims around Lewis. A corrupt don, an old girlfriend, Turnbull's widow, a bicycle through a bookshop window. Lewis is seen to smile and given a few dislikes, namely professional northeners, Oxford colleges (preferred prisons), celebrity criminals, people who wear sunglasses when there is no sunshine, and Barry Manilow.

OXFORD LOCATIONS

Merton College, Front Quadrangle Professor Weller walks across in the rain; women students; Fellows' Garden: walk along wall path. Fitzjames Arch: interview with Professor Weller.

Botanic Garden, lawn by the River Cherwell students on lawn; revolver given.

St Giles and High Street Lewis driving.

Malmaison Hotel: Front area and in converted prison area: student found strangled. Rear plaza: walk from there to front, Turnbull shot, goodnight to Diane.

All Souls College: Aerial view.

Oxford Union, St Michael Street bar: students meet.

St Mary the Virgin Hathaway plays guitar.

Merton Street car tries to run Lewis and Turnbull down. Caroline walking.

High Street, outside church Hathaway notes speeding car.

Path between Merton and Corpus Christi Colleges detectives walk.

Broad Street by Balliol College Lewis and Turnbull walk.

Magdalen Bridge night-time punting.

Magpie Lane Harvey running.

OTHER LOCATIONS

Lewis's flat Flat 2, 10 Gordon Road, Ealing, SW13. Diane stays. Later gives hug and kiss.

Police Station and morgue QinetiQ building, 124 Chobham Lane, Longcross, Chertsey, Surrey. Mrs Turnbull arrives, Lewis smiles.

Blackwell's Bookshop, High Holborn, London bicycle thrown through window.

Duke of Kent Public House, Scotch Common, Ealing Lewis and Diane Turnbull dine.

Gymnasium: Hathaway talks with David Harvey.

Latchmere House Resettlement Prison, Ham Common, Surrey Lewis hears about former inmates.

3   EXPIATION

SERIES 1   4TH MARCH 2007
WRITER   GUY ANDREWS
DIRECTOR   DAN REED

SUMMARY

Two couples who live in Summertown, A and B, go on holiday and swap spouses
and children, as is usual in Summertown. Wife A, Rachel, has a terrible childhood
secret, known to her husband A, David, but unknown to new partner B, Hugh.
Rachel is spooked by Jane Templeton, who knows about her misdeed, and
confesses to Hugh, who is enraged and strangles her, simulating suicide. He then
kills Jane, again attempting to simulate suicide, at which he is not very good.
When his wife B, Louise, now with David, says that they want David's children
back, he hits her and takes the children, and is only prevented from killing them
by our heroes.

Lewis smells a rat from the start, and could have cleared it up earlier if Hugh's
alibi had not been supported, extraordinarily, by two witnesses. There is a blind
don, Le Plassiter, whose function is to provide an excuse for the obligatory college
scenes. The detectives take the usual unlikely strolls through Oxford. Lewis gets
a couple of kisses from Stephanie, but not from his female superintendent who
is unreasonably horrible to him and demotes Hathaway, until Lewis threatens to
resign. We learn that Lewis does not like public speaking but does like Hathaway.

OXFORD LOCATIONS

Exeter College dining hall, Fellows' Garden, Old Gatehouse: Le Plassiter's
college.

Radcliffe Square floodlit walk with Stephanie.

Magdalen College School, playing field and Cherwell bridge dodgy
headmaster.

The Plain view.

Merton Field view.

Portobello Restaurant, 7 South Parade, Summertown, Oxford shortened
dinner date.

Museum of Natural History and Pitt Rivers Museum where Hugh takes
the children and tries to jump from the tower.

The Victoria Arms, Mill Lane, Old Marston Lewis and Hathaway bond (just
like with Morse).

OTHER LOCATIONS

Mallory's house 28 Woodville Gardens, Ealing London.
Stephanie's house 26 Woodville Gardens.
Hayward's house 67 Sheldon Avenue, London N6.
Jane Templeton's house 64 Little Green Lane, Chertsey, Surrey.
Le Plassiter's room Dorney Court, Dorney, Slough.
Police Station QinetiQ building, 124 Longcross, Chertsey, Surrey.
Supermarket Sainsbury's, Lake End Road, Taplow, Berks: interviews Stocker.
Opticians internal receptionist, in love, supports Hugh's alibi. QinetiQ building (above).
Opticians external Whitby & Co., 20 Fleet Street, London, EC4Y.
Forensic Laboratory St Peter's Hospital Mortuary, Chertsey.
Caroline Croft's consulting room Valley End Road, Chobham, Surrey.

4 AND THE MOONBEAMS KISSED THE SEA

SERIES 2	24TH FEBRUARY 2008
WRITER	ALAN PLATER
DIRECTOR	DAN REED

SUMMARY

Conspirators fall out over the forgery of documents by the poet Shelley, stolen from the Bodleian Library. The detectives are given plenty of good humorous lines by Alan Plater's screenplay. There is student tourist guide who fabricates stories; as though that could ever happen! It is just like old Morse times to have another murdering professor. Is Lewis edging closer to Dr Laura Hobson?

LOCATIONS

Oxford Greyhound Stadium, Sandy Lane Chapman gambles and loses.
Seminar Room Harpsden Court, Henley-on-Thames.
River scenes (repeating) Ferry Lane, Mill End, Henley-on-Thames.
Magdalen College cloisters College scene.
Police Station (repeating) QinetiQ building, Longcross, Surrey.
Hobson's party 22 Elm Grove Road, Ealing W5.
Stringer's house 3 Elm Grove Road.
Student's house 6 Corfton Road, Ealing W5.
Magdalen College School white bridges over River Cherwell Nell Buckley and a crocodile.
Schools Quadrangle, Bodleian Library Approach to library
Bodleian Library underground tunnel with body
Turf Tavern Nell's tourist group.
New College Lane, Hertford Bridge Nell talks about spies.
Radcliffe Square continuation of tour.
Quod Bar, High Street Stringer and Walters watch Nell.
Betting shop Fleming and Smith Ltd, Fauconberg Road, Chiswick, W4.
Oxford Botanic Garden detectives meet Mrs Chapman.
Corpus Christi College sundial and Front Quadrangle and seminar room.
Bodleian Library room (repeating) rules of library.
Merton Street detectives walk.
Corpus Christi on roof.
Turf Tavern Lewis on phone.
University College, Radcliffe Quadrangle (repeating) detectives walk to see Dr Walters.
New College Lane aerial view.
Art School University College for the Creative Arts, Falkner Road, Farnham, Surrey.

Earl of Pembroke's statue, Schools Quadrangle, Bodleian General scenes
New College garden Lewis walks with Dr Hobson.
Vaults cafe, University Church, Radcliffe Square General scenes
Corpus Christi cloisters General scenes
St Mary's Church, Turville, near Henley-on-Thames General scenes
University College Shelley Memorial General scenes

Lewis and Hathaway. (Courtsey ITV plc)

5   MUSIC TO DIE FOR

SERIES 2	2ND MARCH 2008
WRITER	DUSTY HUGHES
DIRECTOR	BILL ANDERSON

SUMMARY

A former Stasi informer in East Berlin, now in Oxford, attempts to prevent new incriminating evidence being known. There is a sub-plot of illegal boxing and confused academics. Lewis displays a surprising knowledge of German and Wagner, and it was Morse that caused it all in the first place!

LOCATIONS

Bowers Lock, River Wey, Bowers Lane, Guildford, Surrey river and lock Cole and Helm take a boat trip.

Examination School, High Street Oxford University Boxing Club.

Blackwells Music Shop, Broad Street Valli's workplace.

Trinity College tutorial.

Alderbourne Farm, Alderbourne Lane, Iver, Bucks farm for illegal boxing; police raid.

Sackler Library, Ashmolean Museum, St John Street exterior Portobello Club.

Portobello Club interior Cobden Club, 170 Kensal Road, London W10.

Lewis's flat Flat 2, 10 Gordon Road, Ealing W5.

Helm's house The River House, 52, Strand on the Green, London W4 Cole killed.

Trinity College (Saville College) dining hall and rear of Portobello Club.

Police Station, hospital QinetiQ building, 124 Chobham Lane, Longcross, Surrey.

Trinity College Grove, Garden Quad and Durham Quad.

Trinity College Cole's study

Boxing club locker room Bisham Abbey National Sports Centre, Bisham, Marlow, Bucks.

Examination School exterior.

Ann Kreil's house 88 Fulmer Drive, Gerrards Cross, Bucks.

Trinity College, front quad Jack cycles.

Radcliffe Square and Catte Street Jack and Milo quarrel.

Holywell Music Room, Holywell Street exterior Dimmitus offices.

Bath Place and St Helens Passage Ann followed.

Trinity Milo and Helm meet.

Blackwells Music Shop, Broad Street Lewis interviews Valli.

Radcliffe Square detectives talk.

River Cherwell, Botanic Garden Helm in electric-powered boat.

Alexanderplatz, Berlin Berlin scenes

Ryan Gallen's flat 11 Grenville Court, Kent Avenue, Ealing W13.

Pathology Lab St Peter's Hospital mortuary, Chertsey, Surrey.

Valli's flat The Cedars, Heronsforde, London W13.

Portobello Club interior Cobden Club, 170 Kensal Road, London W10; recital.

Acre's house Flat 2, The Sports Club, Park View Road, London.

Berlin and Brandenberg Gate & Stasi Archive interior Rennie House, Rennie Street, London SE1.

Broad Street and Sheldonian Theatre Scenes

Denys Wilkinson Building, Keble Road hospital.

New College Lane Helms meet.

Botanic Garden, River Cherwell Scenes

Police Station Scenes

Bowers Lock, River Wey, Bowers Lane, Guildford, Surrey River and lock; cast assembles.

Kriel's House Scenes

Lewis's flat Morse's letter.

6 LIFE BORN OF FIRE

SERIES 2	9TH MARCH 2008
WRITER	TOM MACRAE
DIRECTOR	RICHARD SPENSE

SUMMARY

A dark tale involving five assorted deaths, and almost six, Hathaway's, in which his religious past, and a callous rejection, return to haunt him. Along the way homophobia, organised religion and viewer credibility are put to the test, as a vengeful and remarkably resourceful killer plays with fire, and the special effects men have their day at last.

LOCATIONS

St Thomas's Church St Mary and All Saints, Windsor End, Beaconsfield, Bucks.

Interior Communion Club Mary Magdalene Church, Rowington Close, London W2.

Dr Melville's Hospice Walpole House, Waldegrave Road, Strawberry Hill, Middlesex.

Exeter College detectives meet Mr McKewan.

Radcliffe Square and Brasenose College exterior Mayfield College.

Botanic Garden Jonjo jogging.

McKewan's house 10 Woodville Gardens, Ealing W5.

King Edward Street Jonjo's flat exterior.

Interior Sadie's and Jonjo's House 10 Woodville Gardens, Ealing.

Revd King's house 7 North Common Road, Ealing, W5.

Hathaway's flat 144 Percy Road, Shepherds Bush, London, W12.

Allotments Ranelagh Road, Ealing, London.

Brasenose College Jonjo films Lady Hugh.

Police Station QinetiQ building, 124 Chobham Lane, Longcross, Surrey.

Merton Street and exterior Merton College Lewis meets Charlie Newton, reporter.

Church garden cafe Beaconsfield.

St Thomas's Church St Mary and All Saints; Hathaway meets Zoe then Jonjo.

Radcliffe Square Gay demonstration; Lewis escorts Lady Hugh into Brasenose, emerge in Lincoln College: Front Quadrangle and warden's office.

Crematorium Putney Vale, Stag Lane, London SW15.

Merton Street Lewis is suspicious.

Brasenose College Lewis meets Nova Rose.

Interior Communion Club Mary Magdalene Church, Rowington Close, London W2.

Radcliffe Square Jonjo films and hassles Lady Hugh.

Brasenose College Lady Hugh killed.

Catte Street Jonjo and Hathaway talk about love and bells.

Broad Street; The Buttery Conan at cafe.

Sheldonian Theatre and Clarendon Building exterior.

Botanic Garden with Zoe Kenneth.

Turl Bar, Turl Street march reaches pub.

Gay Pride Pub interior The Rose and Crown, Church Place, St Mary's Road, Ealing W5.

New College Lane Lewis and Hathaway argue post-Gay Pride march.

Interior Will's flat 28 Hamilton Road, Ealing.

31 Nelson Street, Jericho Zoe's house.

Interior Zoe's House Stage R, Shepperton Studios, Middlesex.

Hospital QinetiQ building, 124 Chobham Lane, Longcross, Surrey.

Allotment and Radcliffe Square General scenes

7   THE GREAT AND THE GOOD

SERIES 2	16TH MARCH 2008
WRITER	PAUL RUTMAN
DIRECTOR	STUART ORME

SUMMARY

Rumour has it that this was the most problematical episode to bring to the screen, with filming delayed. It was a complicated plot, the deciphering of which the average viewer would have been behind the detectives, who in turn would have been trailing behind the screenwriter. We are asked to believe that a group of prominent men would put their trust in one man to provide them with alibis while they performed misdeeds. Of course it all goes pear-shaped, but there is a genuine murderous academic to compensate! Lewis's dead wife pops up again, and he gets no further than analysing corpses with the improbably lovely Dr Hobson. The last two episodes of this series take us back to the suburb of Jericho, where *Morse* started twenty-three years ago.

LOCATIONS

River Meadow (as Port Meadow, Jericho) Warren Lane, Pyrford, Surrey.
Meadow car park Copas estate, Medmenham, Marlow, Bucks.
Hospital Ashford Hospital, Middlesex.
Power Plant WRG Appleford Sidings, Sutton Courtenay.
Adebayou's office Ravenscourt Park Hospital, Hammersmith.
School Haydon School, Wiltshire Lane, Pinner.
Turl Street detectives drink coffee.
Ashton's house Principal's lodgings, Hertford College.
Police Station QinetiQ building, 124 Chobham Lane, Longcross, Surrey.
Donnelly's house 50 Minsterley Avenue, Upper Halliford, Surrey.
Cooper's flat 19 Leamington Road Villas, Notting Hill, London.
Catte Street detectives talk.
Oxford Tutorial College, King Edward Street Local radio station.
BBC Radio Oxford, Banbury Road, Summertown Local radio station (interior).
Oriel Square and College interview Gavin Matthews.
Matthews' house 9 Riverdale Road, Twickenham.
Police cell Rickmansworth Police Station, Rectory Road.
Ashmolean Museum Beaumont Street, art exhibition.
Magpie Lane Sporetti reads letter.
Pub (as Bookbinders' Arms) The Seven Stars, Newark Lane, Ripley, Surrey.
Lewis's flat Eastgate Hotel, Merton Street.
Cafe exterior AMT Coffee, Cornmarket/Ship Street.
Broad Street Ashton jogging.
Cooper's flat (and opposite) Jericho Street, Walton Crescent.

ACKNOWLEDGEMENTS

The compilation of this guide has only been possible with the generous inspiration and support of too many people and reference books to fully name; my apologies to those overlooked.

Colin Dexter, for generous support, Philip Pullman for encouragement, Isobel Gillan, patiently accommodating text changes until the last minute. Matthew Morgan, top Oxford photographer. Nick Lockett, Head of Pictures/Carlton Television, not only for the Morse and Lewis photos. Belinda Wright and Kevin Whately, Derek Webster and Sheila Hancock, for permission to use the photos. Russell Lodge and Denis Firminger, Locations Managers for the series. Anne Gallagher, Tourist Information Officer, Oxford City Council. Fellow guides including Ted East, former Marshal of the University, for advice on Town Vs Gown and Pennie Chalmers for advice on the music. The staff at EdenIco, designers of The Inspector Morse Collection. Virginia Green, former PA to Kenny McBain. Bob Maher, manager of The Trout Inn, Wolvercote. David Bishop, author of *The Complete Inspector Morse*, for painstaking analysis, *The Encyclopaedia of Oxford* by Christopher and Edward Hibbert.

Extra special thanks to Lindsay Siviter, friend of the makers and stars of the series, deviser of the *Morse* exhibition at the Oxford Town Museum, historian, 'No. 1 Morse fan', and presently Assistant Curator at the Sheldonian Theatre. Having seen the proofs, she writes: *This is a well researched, highly informative and enjoyable guide to Morse's Oxford, essential reading for all Morse fans. It provides, amongst other things, exciting, hitherto unpublished, knowledge of many Morse locations – fantastic! Simply a must for all Morse enthusiasts.*

Also, many thanks to Matt Clarke, location manager for *Lewis*.

IN APPRECIATION

In the real world: of Colin Dexter, author, script advisor, kind contributor to this guide and cameo actor; Ted Childs and the late Kenny McBain of Central Television; Anthony Minghella and Julian Mitchell, founder screen writers; the late John Thaw, Kevin Whateley and James Grout who created enduring characters; Dr Robert Gasser of Brasenose College who helped bring Oxford to the world.

In the parallel universe of *Inspector Morse*: to over 100 citizens who died for the cause, about seventy-three of whom were murdered; to about thirty men and elevenwomen who committed unnecessarily interesting murders and demanded so little proof before giving themselves up; to a succession of pathologists who delighted in Morse's discomfort at their trade; to the twenty-one ladies Morse hesitatingly pursued, mostly with scant success; to Chief Inspector Endeavour Morse; Detective Sergeant Robbie Lewis and Chief Superintendent Strange, who seldom showed how much they liked each other.

Finally, to a unique series that attracted an audience across social and national boundaries, to the delight of advertisers.

ABOUT THE AUTHOR

Bill Leonard is a member of The Oxford Guild of Guides and a Blue Badge guide, and has been conducting *Inspector Morse* tours in Oxford and the surrounding area since 1996. He has acted as a consultant to Eden-co, designers of the 'Complete Collection' magazines. All the drawings have been prepared by the author.

The author.

If you are interested in purchasing other books published by The History Press, or in case you have difficulty finding any of our books in your local bookshop, you can also place orders directly through our website

www.thehistorypress.co.uk